NOT QUITE POSTHUMOUS LETTER TO MY DAUGHTER

By the same Author:

LEFTOVER LIFE TO KILL

CAITLIN THOMAS

* * * * * * *

NOT QUITE POSTHUMOUS LETTER TO MY DAUGHTER

An Atlantic Monthly Press Book

LITTLE, BROWN AND COMPANY
BOSTON TORONTO

LIBRARY OF CONGRESS CATALOG CARD NO. 63-8964

FIRST AMERICAN EDITION

ATLANTIC–LITTLE, BROWN BOOKS
ARE PUBLISHED BY
LITTLE, BROWN AND COMPANY
IN ASSOCIATION WITH
THE ATLANTIC MONTHLY PRESS

PRINTED IN THE UNITED STATES OF AMERICA

NOT QUITE
POSTHUMOUS LETTER
TO MY DAUGHTER

I

My Dear Little Daughter,

You are not really so little as all that, I know, since you have just had your eighteenth birthday on the third of March. But, like all real mothers since the world began, I still think of you as little: and the sweetest thing that God ever made. Although you are probably a lot bigger than I am now, since I am shrinking as fast as you are growing. Bigger, and stronger without a doubt, in every present thing. With the exclusion only of the past things that time alone can teach one: and takes a jolly long time to make them sink in; that I hope to teach you, now that you are starting out in life.

Because I could not bear to see you floundering in the same mudbath of experience that very nearly submerged me altogether; and has left me the delinquent wreck I am today. I literally believed all that romantic claptrap about the imperativeness of sinking to the bottom for the sake of spiritual enrichment. You may not believe I could be so fantastically daft, but there was no limit to my daftness: nor Dylan's either, for that matter, in those days. But fortunately, in your sober generation, such bohemian licence: of imagining that every orgy of excess is permitted to the Artist; not to mention the Genius; is absurdly out of date. And fortunately in your case, with the Catholic religion to uphold you, and the flaming examples of your parents before your eyes, there are no danger signals as yet of your being sucked down into any such degradation of false conceptions. But it is as well to be meticulously prepared, and fully armed, for whatever threats to your resistance may come along.

When I say a real mother, I obviously don't mean a good mother: I mean a mother who, however bad she is, puts her young fiercely before everybody else. Whose love for them is not the sentimental thing that civilized love suggests; but more like the possessive fury of a beast in the jungle. With a potent element of wonder thrown in: wonder at her production of them.

And, since I was born under the sign of Sagittarius – which must represent, in my case, not half horse and half man, but half mare and half mother – and also on the day of the Immaculate Conception, it is inevitable that my most powerful instincts are maternal.

Since I have also now reached the age when I have positively not an eyelash of physical vanity left: my clackers can rattle down to my flat feet and my wig drop off in front of the howling mob for all I care; I therefore propose to give you the benefit of what I have learned through spreading my meat on the waters and collecting the bones. Bones which, at this precise moment, I am sitting up in bed chewing over.

So I want to save you from making the same mistake as I did: of spreading your meat on the waters. . . . But instead, to store it in the deep freeze and eke it out, cut by bloody cut. Till it is seductively high, and ready to fetch the most profitable price from the highest bidder. No ridiculous sentiment will be allowed to mar our relentless scheme of calculated climbing into the moneyed Mansions: never mind the class, they are too poor nowadays. After that, once in, there will be plenty of time to do a bit of spreading . . . and be as flamboyant as you like. Besides, it is more remuneratively effective to do the spitting and crashing from the inside: rather than from the outside abortively spitting and crashing in.

So, if you wish to become, as I devoutly wish you to become, having never made it myself, the whipped cream of the Bourgeoisie; and to capture that mythical millionaire whom I never managed to capture: whom we have now firmly planted in mercenary singleness of mind for once; please listen very carefully to my matured advice and mellow words of warning.

But I need not tell you again for a start, that if we are to make this delicate penetration into the genteel realms of respectability: which is a necessary operation at this stage; you must be the diametrical opposite of what I have been and what I have done. For you have already instinctively understood that painful point very thoroughly: with a child's callous condemnation of its parents' wrongs. You may perhaps accuse me of boasting of my wrongs, but I do assure you, dear, they are far too ignominious to boast about. For they rise up out of the night, when I am not on the look-out, and poke under my sleeping defending elbows, with vicious prods in the belly. Perhaps my greatest wrong was putting you children before Dylan, instead of trying with all my guts to keep him from the dogs. But then I was as much in need of reforming as he, and revelled with him among the dogs. So, although you know that the last thing I want to do is to interfere with your religion, it is no good telling me that Hell is in the hereafter. For I am prepared to swear that it is here on this bleeding Earth, and nowhere else. And Heaven too. But Heaven is much more elusive, like all the rest of the flying skyward bodies.

There was too, in that frivolous age, a trivially crazy idea that it was *clever* to drink to extinction; and *clever* to be promiscuous to dulling the discrimination of the flesh. Which gave a mock glamour to these tawdry occupations;

and people who did neither were considered unutterably drab and boring. When we know perfectly well, luckily, that the reverse is the truth. But I seemed to be hypnotized by these wrongs, for they had but to say the magic words: do wrong; and I, like a blind idiot, obediently: did wrong. And it is this accumulation of wrongs that is the reason for me finding myself, at this late date, in the identical squalor of despair that I started out in. Not having raised myself by so much as an aspidistra, or a potted palm, into the enviable ranks of accepted uniformity.

Surrounded always by an ancient miscellaneous collection of disgusting old junk, of repulsive objects, of foul abandonments piled up in every verminous corner of the hopelessly sagging room. The sordid confusion, the brainstorms of print, dominated by sad battalions of heel-downed boat-worn shoes; defeated regiments of empty reproving bottles.

So that even the impulse to brush up the dissolute mess, with a fluff-clogged broom into a grime-sodden dustpan, evaporates at birth. This kind of squalid poverty may be tolerable, even beneficial for a limited time in youth: for everybody should know, through suffering it, what poverty means; but, if it goes on too long, it pulls down the spirit and stultifies the soul, so that even the impulse to move out of it gets blocked. And, with age, one tends to wrap one's misery around one, for fear that this last threadbare blanket will be taken away too.

Never make the unpardonable error, then, of thinking that it is romantic to be poor. For youth, which has the riches of health, it is less important; but for age, which has lost them, it is all-essential to compensate with artificial riches.

So let this be your first chastening lesson on what must not be: on what must be radically changed. Let your burning preoccupation be to get us out of this squalor dump: that I have so abysmally failed to get us out of. Let us single-mindedly concentrate on the material betterment of our domestic and social position.

For, far from becoming more spiritual as one gets older as is generally supposed, I have become a caterwauling virago of fanatical materialism. A dedicated cash-counter in the cellar by candlelight: Uriah Heep isn't in it, I can tell you.

I can see clearly now the perfect logic of Granny Thomas's suggestion: in our newly-married barmily balmy days sponging on her in the Tight provinces; that we should put by half a crown a week to be buried tidy. Though we were superbly indignant, of course, at that moneyless time. When one has no money one can despise it with a free untrammelled conscience. But ever since, I have been busily totting up how many half-crowns would have accumulated had I had the Welsh sense to take her advice. Incidentally, it might not be a bad idea if you started thinking about being buried tidy . . . But Dylan escaped early from such mercenary beggings, having always said he would; and laughed at the inconsistency of us ever diminishing into a couple of bent-double, gout-ridden, toothless, drooling, bald crocks: against all the laws of beautiful nature. Leaving me to prove the survival of the ninth of November fool: and that a bone head lasts longer than a head of consuming fire.

But all this background of nostalgia: of estuary, birds and tidal mists, which is more like a landscape of the heart than one of mud and sea and cockles; which has penetrated into your childhood being as deeply as it has into my grown-up being, constituting the core of our combined memories: this home of heavenly dimensions in retrospect; we must ruthlessly put behind us. For it hurts too much to go back; everything seems shrunk, mildewed, skeleton lonely: as though even the ghosts had gone out of it. One should never go back to a place one has loved; for, however rough the going forward is, it is better than the snuffing out-of-love return.

So always think of tomorrow. I used to think it would never come, but My God it did: like being slapped in the stomach with a flat-fish; and keep planning and pipe-dreaming about our new life . . . whether it comes off or not, for the fantasy is, often as not, more fun than the fact: and all we have got so far is the fantasy. That's the way people keep going in prison: or how could they ever stand the bleak repetition of imprisoned actions getting nowhere.

However, as you know, I have great faith in you, for what with the pure Thomas looks: and the Thomas breed goes back to God knows what original bogs; that is to say, curly hair, bumpy forehead, frog eyes, voluptuous-to-be mouth, *and* an expression of ingenuous innocence: who said it was not genuine; concealing a cauldron of fiends: of egotism, perversity and capriciousness, that I am bound to admit come from my hateful character: but nevertheless a scratch of bitchery in a woman is a necessity if she is to be noticed; there will be no stopping you.

This miniature feminine version of Dylan, without the blowing-up-blowsiness of debauchery attached: it would be just too bad if it were; fills me with a conflict of tenderness and frustration. For, with all your outward semblance of him, you still are not your father.

I am afraid most of Dylan's charming disposition, and gregariousness with all types of people, must have gone into your brothers. But it is just as well because a woman has always got to be much tougher than a man: while simulating the fragility of dainty Dresden china; or how would she do all the dirty work that she inevitably has to do.

But each one of us in the family have unanimously suffered from that unfinished look of a premature birth; from the same shaming Celtic shyness which we desperately try to cover up with a load of false bombast; and from a prodigiously slow development into maturity. A maturity that Dylan missed out altogether: he refused to grow up because the responsibility of it was too cumbersome for him. And a maturity that I am only slowly coming to now; because you know what a prize tortoise of slowness I am in every laborious thing I do.

It is a lot nicer than I expected, being mature: lying back in a tepid bath, watching others for a change pulling out the world by the roots. Instead of tearing at it myself with a starved hyena's teeth.

But you are still at the tearing stage, and must naturally experiment. With moderation and circumspection however, keeping our fiends of destruction scrupulously sealed up. And, since you are as adept at putting on an Act as I was: impersonating a different exotic film star every week, though nobody would know it; and anybody would think you were a perfect angel and model of behaviour: for they are always telling me, to my amazement, how lucky I am to have such a wonderful little help about the house; I think we will have no difficulty, between us, in plugging the blind of virtue over unsuspecting eyes.

Roly Poly Pudding and Pie.
Sugar And Spice And All Things Nice.

That's our Granny's Girl Angel Cake Act. Works like a recipe for charm every public duping time. For as long as you can keep spreading your artificial layers of jam: against your natural grain. For as long as you can preserve your icing cream top uncracked.

Until the trying strain of play-acting: Dainty Dolly Does It; cracks the superficial farce wide open. And your Tiger Filling: banished in the basement for the occasion, and clawing at the walls to get out; spills out uproariously.

Takes over your sham sweetness; your candy ball of modesty and docility: rolled together on syrup dripping toast; your fresh innocent pat of still unmelted butter in your honey-bunched mouth; and swallows the putrid lot whole. With not so much as a peek-a-boo of resistance out of you.

Without the merest atomic jolt of polite transition, you lightly toss overboard into swiftly devouring space: your well-meaning resolutions, your solemn vows; as airily as ridding yourself of an overload of cumbersome balloon ballast.

And abruptly: before the shocked unbelieving eyes of the company: but not ours; you turn back into your off-stage, unmasked, familiar creature. Better known to your long suffering familiars, in the ungarnished privacies of the wrangle-resounding house, as: 'Bubble And Squeak, Plus Green Welsh Leek.' A squaremouthed bucket howling, with mop of Bongo hair on: a Bongo howl of revolt. 'I am I; properly I; I myself. And no fancy bugger else.'

Which is one egging-me-on reason, why I go on so blithely nagging you to no effect whatsoever; and giving you gratis such worldly-wise, heavy mother's advice. In the same certitude that: in the most unlikely accident of you happening to listen, or read it at all; you will, if only as a matter of strong principle, do the obedient contrary.

But if you were the sensitive caring type, like your less omnipotent brothers, I should never dare take the responsibility of opening my woodpecking beak. For, although I am convinced of your hidden mine of inner sensibilities, I have not yet had the privilege of a glimpse at it: through the stratas of granite. Perhaps it will surface later: along with your retarded growing up, and astonished understanding that there are other people who feel in the world: besides yourself. Even if there are a lot more who don't.

Should I venture to warn, however, the devoted supporters of your lily-white loveliness: which is both yours in spite of you, but not yours if you can help it; to look out . . . For, pure and lovely as you are, there nevertheless lurks, within your decoying deception, a character: putting it at its mildest for them; that might, at any minute spring out at them unexpectedly.

The simple word that best sums up my faraway Darling: in the definition of the Concise Oxford Dictionary; is, congruously enough, *rough*. Not wild or quiet or gentle, unrestrained, violent, stormy, boisterous, disorderly, riotous, inconsiderate, harsh, unfeeling, drastic, severe, grating, astringent . . .

Rough music: but equally applicable to your first nursing efforts. Deficient in finish or elaboration or delicacy, incomplete, rudimentary, entirely or partly unwrought, merely passable, inexact, approximate, preliminary . . .

Or again, when applied to *Roughcast*, on wall. Coated with mixture of lime and gravel; not elaborate, just good enough, not over particular, roughly efficient or effective . . . *Rough and tumble*: Irregular, scrambling, disorderly: significantly repeated for you; regardless of procedure rule . . .

Even if you would appear, to distant strangers: as a daisy in a field of thistles.

Only you and I know with a vengeance: that it is you who are the spiked thistle, surrounded by fried egg daisies.

Between ourselves it is the uniquely better tough thing

to be; and your unique chance of survival as a cornered female.

I have a great faith in the rewards of work: more than in any other one specific thing; most especially manual work of any description which uses all the parts of the body harmoniously. Too much thinking work leads to an oppression, a confusion, an exhaustion of the spirit. Through work – from the most menial to the creative, and creative work is largely menial – God grows unconsciously. Because I believe, unlike you, that God is not floating in the ether, but unbudgeably lodged, in differing sizes, in the heads of every single person on the earth. And he grows and responds in exact measure to the amount of work we do for him.

So you, I am glad to say, are not afraid of the smell of work; particularly if it furthers your own interests. To be sure, you are hopelessly untidy, in spite of my ceaselessly telling you, like Samuel Butler, that by tidying up your personal refuse you are tidying up the thoughts in your mind. And you are a hopeless slut in the way you treat your clothes, flinging them all over the place, like discarded rags to be trampled on: as though you were a born princess who had but to lift a tapering finger for a bevy of slaves to appear with fresh raiment. In other words, for your downtrodden mother to come and automatically pick them up.

But these deplorable habits will eventually be cured, I trust, when you come to realize that fastidiousness of person and possessions is a reflection of fastidiousness of soul. For when have you ever seen your lovely nuns looking slovenly. The immaculateness of their interiors demands an immaculate exterior.

And I have a great loathing for waste: probably because I have been the greatest waster of all time since going to pot in pubs. Since living in a continual state of disreputable chaos. Due to lack of training, lack of discipline, and lack of any specific skill to keep me in a protective routine, a pattern of order. So, in revulsion against our perpetual disorder, I bitterly hate deliberate waste which is synonymous with mental carelessness. Though, Heaven knows, nobody could call me stingy, for I was the ostentatious reverse. Always the big hospitable gesture, whether broke or not, seeing myself as an all-embracing Goddess of bountiful generosity. But no more: never no more; at least I have cut out that form of self-flattery.

When I think of the agonizing hours of unadulterated boredom I have spent in dull as ditchwater pubs with Dylan: to preserve his sacred drinking myth; longing for green fields in which to roll away my impurities; drinking drinks I didn't want at all: my first thought in the morning then was: *What* shall I drink today? till out of sheer habit and the necessity to transform the blankness of reality, I began to really want drink: worse still, not to be able to do without it; when I think of all that waste of time, money, and talent, I could cry with exasperation at our pettiness. When, at our serious roots, neither of us was a petty person.

When I think of how enormously strong I was, how crackling with life: and all that boundless energy sucked down the drains of dissipation . . . I am maddened by this tragic crime of wasted potentialities. And now so despicably weak that I am not even fit to take the job of lavatory attendant, for fear of bungling the change. As you once kindly suggested to me as an ultimate soporific kill-time.

I try to convince myself that this rollicking in theory, jollificating as a duty, verbal spewing of distorted words into unlistening space; this bad, unproductive boozing time was not entirely wasted. As I try to convince myself that the lengthy periods of seeming inertia, with the will in passive abeyance: in illness, in imprisonment, in artistic disgust of work for instance; must serve some useful purpose. That the living deaths in public institutions, in private rooms, can't be utterly senseless. For I refuse to accept that anything can be for nothing.

But there is no concrete evidence to prove the hidden fertility in these deserts of apathy. Except the passion with which I tell you now to beware of the evils, the weakness, the cowardice of drink. The waste of talk, and the waste of company. It is a mere dispersion of the personality. A necessary dispersion perhaps at the beginning: on the way to finding yourself.

So never depend on immersion in another person for your personal growth: for the creation of your real personality: for the other person is merely preying on you to create their own. As you are preying on them, agreed, whether you wish to or not. As we naturally prey one upon the other for the compensatory food we need. So don't listen to those tall tales of their sacrificing their all for you; for they sacrifice but to gain what they desire more. But only through yourself alone will you eventually achieve wholeness.

I don't think I can hammer into you much more at the moment on the evils of drink: though there is plenty more that could be said, believe me. But remember that evil, to be a potent temptation, must be pleasurable. Must be disguised at least in the illusion of pleasure. But the true evil of drink lies in the disillusion: that the initial pleasure very soon evaporates, leaving a demoralizing craving for more, which is not even temporarily pleasurable. Which then leads to deterioration of the faculties of both body and mind; plus a bewildering lack of co-operation between the two.

The third D, after demoralization and deterioration, is the ghastly degradation that besets its helpless victims afterwards: at some later time of guilty reckoning. A degradation so insupportable that, in order to wipe it out, they are impelled to rush for the bottle again. And so it goes on in the infamous, viciously compelling circle.

As for the weakness and cowardice of drink: they are not necessarily present originally in the character of the person who drinks. They are another of drink's unnatural, below-the-belt, creations. For by so weakening the drinker he forcibly becomes cowardly.

But there is an important point here that I think you should not lose sight of: that an artist, who is usually a person of violent extremes, of violent excesses, must have, not the strength of a normal man to create; but to be able to create through the constant counter-attacks of drink, a super strength of determination. That, since it is a thousand times tougher to work in spite of drink, he must be a super tough to do it. That is what your father was: a super tough, till the drink got tougher than he was.

That is why I am determined that the drink will not get tougher than me; which is not to say, with all my noble talk of reform, that I will stop drinking; but that I will try to moderate it to my capacity. To take just as much as my feeble frame can stand, without passing out. For I am not yet quite prepared to die. I must add too: though this is not to encourage the habit, mind; that I personally still infinitely prefer drinking people to the smug virtue of the bouncingly healthy disapprovers of drink. To the unimaginative pomposity of the non-drinkers, who simply can't imagine why anybody should be so pathetic as to deliberately do something which they know will do them harm. Pathetic, in the sense of failure to arrive in the golden ports of success, perhaps; but how much more human, more sympathetic, and immeasurably funnier than the know-alls who do arrive. Whose golden arrival seems to shear them of the wool of humanity, dock their tails of charity, and clip their heads of humour. So panic-stricken are they to defend, against all impostors, their precious privileges.

But I have lived too long, I fear, among down and out, odd neurotic, freakish eccentric, queer mixtures of misfits like myself: to feel at home or happy among up and in, smooth and sleek, polished and plump, all alike penguins of fitting-in convention.

It is different for you, who, having never been properly down and out, we are consequently pushing, as hard as we can, up and in. Then you can tell me what it is really like up there. It is bound to be amusing, intriguing, scandalous once you get behind that penguin bib. For society dons that diplomatic uniform to screen its flagrant indiscretions. And, once you are impregnably established, I can sneak in the back door and get a gloating eyeful through a hole in the attic floor. Some people, like padded Oscar Wilde, prefer to be on the inside of society: looking out. But I prefer to be, like skinned Van Gogh, on the outside of society: looking in.

To see and not to be seen, through all the shuttered windows on all the social levels: the private intimacies enacted with no audience; has always been my unrealizable ambition of curiosity. I don't want the responsibility of participating, for then one sees nothing. Mine is simply the passion for seeing, for knowing.

To be the dynamic mistress of your fate is what essentially matters; instead of letting your fate dictate to you what is to be done. To be enslaved by a personal relationship, for instance: which is an enslavement of the will to act independently: by a vice like drink which has made itself indispensable, or by the tyranny of too much money over too little money; is an intolerable humiliation.

But to decide of your own free will to be self-enslaved; to voluntarily choose a low and humble position, as the religious lunatics do, is not only tolerable, but a proud humiliation. The difference being that it has been your own pride of choice, as opposed to having the lowliness insultingly thrust upon you in spite of you. The confinement of a convent as opposed to the confinement of a prison camp.

Your confinement: since confinement of some sort is unavoidable if we are to make a logical shape out of your life; will be, we trust, in the moneyed Mansions; which are equally confined, make no mistake; but by the exclusive laws of money. Excluding all that is superfluous to the exclusiveness that money represents.

I would advise a recent amasser of a slathering heap of mint-new money: rather than the old class of traditional amasser of a hereditary fortune: because this loud vulgar type, as he is called, likes to spend, to show off and enjoy his newfound wealth. Whereas, with the refined indifference of the habitual money holder, goes a congenital streak of acute meanness. Which no doubt accounts for him holding on to it for so long. He will write a reluctant cheque when positively forced to do so; but it is far too clumsy for him to carry loose jingling coins in his pockets. So his poor companion with no bank account automatically pays the taxi and hands over cash for tips which are never reimbursed. For a man of distinction is above considering such paltry expenditure; and, on such embarrassing occasions, his abstract attention is riveted on some distant point of the horizon.

But, as for me, since being accustomed to Dylan's crooked world of bouncing cheques, I have developed a grave mistrust of them: nearly always rightly so. For where is the half-wit who will cash them.

So hold on tight every time to the strutting peasant with bulging money bags strung all about his ostentatious person; for his lack of blue breeding will be amply compensated for by his native kindliness. A lot of warm vulgarity is incomparably preferable to a little bit of pinched niceness.

I am not referring to the peasants who remain in the fields, for they are as craftily mean as the aristocrats can be. Nor am I talking about the exceptions to the rule, for there are exceptional Scotchmen and Jews, after all.

But, if that whiskered rat Hitler has done nothing else praiseworthy, he has now made it our Holy duty to love the Jews as an entire race. Whereas before one might have loved one and loathed another. Just as it becomes our Holy duty to love the entire race of coloured people when they are persecuted. For they cease then to be individuals and are massed together into principles: into the snobbish Holiness, however awful one member may be, with which they are invested today. A snobbish *must* at all the fashionable meeting places. But better an exaggerated adulation than the vilery of blood discrimination anyhow.

But this tirade smacks too much of politics to be comfortably digestible; and politics, as everybody ought to know, are the most boring subjects on earth: causing the ears of the listener to snap shut with an involuntary click. The reason being, I think, that they are a biased playing off of one prejudice against another so that one never gets at the basic truth underneath. Certainly not a fit feminine subject; so be very careful never to get launched, on a gust of hot air, discussing politics . . . It will only put you in a boiling temper, in an unsuitable light, and in a worse muddle, if not murder, than you were already.

Besides, we must remember, though it is difficult at times, that we are women with no opinions: and such manly discussions belong to men.

So let us revert to the universal subject of money, which is as dear to the hearts of women as it is to men. Although the 'best people' don't mention money; for it is easy not to mention when there is enough of it. I think I should here briefly mention: never pretending to be one of the 'best people'; the smell of corruption that follows money wherever it goes. And the peril of being so influenced by it, that it amounts to a pernicious worship of the stuff.

No such deification of it has ever bothered us, nor I think ever will; for we suffer from the reverse: treating it with too little respect. Which is why we never have enough and always want more.

So let us try and be a little more respectful to its piling up powers; to recognize that, while it is supremely desirable, it is still not a divine thing. And to never omit, however great the gratification of its gifts, to keep a good gob of contempt in reserve at the back of the throat.

Like a lot of supremely desirable things, when one has *not* got them; when one does get them, one forgets all about them, and begins to desire an alternatively supremely desirable thing.

However, money tops the list for both the rich and poor. For the rich in order to retain their standard of living, for the poor in order to live. Shall we say that it is a shade more vital for the poor.

Because of the importance of money and the adulation it brings; and also because of the good a plodding occupation does to your moral character; I am determined you shall learn a trade of a nice solid wage-earning kind. No matter how dull; and harbour your inner strength and future potentialities as jealously as pearls in an oyster.

This stodging trade: something as plebeian as a nodding, tapping secretary, but severely aloof; is merely to mark time of course till our decrepit millionaire: because you can't be too fussy about looks, we decided; strolls along and spots you. For the possession of a reputable job: nothing remotely intellectual, for Heaven's sake; creates a favourable impression. Then, as soon as he is well impaled and wriggling upon the hook, you can drop it like a ton of typewriters. And, just in case you don't promptly hook him to his doom, there is always the job to fall back on.

But, whatever you do, do your best to keep away from Art and Artists. Again, you have enough terrible examples there to show you how much progressive use they are, and where they tend to land up: on the dung heap.

So, unless you are irresistibly shoved beyond all human control, to create: pack it in. Let the little buds of creation wither, for lack of cultivation, in the stifling womb. If they dare to pop out their tapeworm heads, cut them crudely back. They will do more harm than good; for there is already a glut of bad creation: and you are not likely to be in the minority of chosen Elect. So, by learning more, you will create: but a desire for more.

It is this initial shove of protest in Art that makes the making of it worth while. All the rest: the gift, the technique, the style; are secondary and suppressible: a mere ornamentation and colouration of the shove. A sacred shove which every true Artist, once he has recognized it, works in perpetual fear of losing. For if circumstances are too heavily loaded against it, he will lose it.

Anyone who has attempted to create knows the hellishness of it, which consists in the final inescapability from it. Knows that anything, however deadly humdrum to drug the senses, is preferable to it. Knows the gigantic effort to get started on the boundless, unwieldy, shapeless material; the forest of hesitations: of what to keep and what to throw out; the running-out terror and reluctance in one of finishing. That there must be a finishing touch to put in, that can't be left out: but what in the devil is it? Or should it be omitted after all?

Then the ghastly going back over the laborious work and seeing how flat, stale, and hopeless it looks: without a grain of life after all the bursting grains that went into it. The sobering conclusion that it is obvious it has got to be done all over again, or chucked out in the dustbin. So rather than tackle that dead duck again, a new sparkling work is started; and later, another carcase is discarded.

As for the proverbial moments of inspiration: there is an occasional fluent lucidity which comes, as it were, through a tunnel, between the jam of stationary traffic in the head and the wide clear road beyond. It comes suddenly, unexpectedly, out of a relenting blue, like a soothing ointment on an angry scar. But these wondrous moments of disbelief: of a door opening from the narrow clogged personality on to the spacious fluid universe; though most satisfactory, are not complete. All too horribly soon the traffic jam is back; and the chronic dissatisfaction of the Artist for whatever he has done, which is never good enough. Never taken out of his grubby hands entirely.

The sweat and blood of labour pains isn't in it; is by comparison a mild bilious attack. So stick, my child, for goodness' sake, to creating babies, washing nappies, and crooning lullabies. For a woman's place, as Dylan never ceased to tell me in vain, is in the bed or at the sink. And the extent of her travels should be from one to the other and back.

Besides, you can always hand your babies over to the doting grandmother; as you know I love such mummified vegetables till they begin to talk: and remind me of the mental awfulnesses of before and to come.

It goes without saying that neither should a woman ever drink, according to Dylan's prehistoric rules; for, as men never tire of driving home, there is nothing worse than a drunken woman. They are probably right from a biological point of view; but they seem to be under some sweet delusion that a drunken man, on the other hand, is clownishly endearing. He generally gets less hysterical, shall we say. But neither is maudlin sentimentality followed by the sick-bowl conducive to romance.

Nor should a woman ever make tedious generalities about Art, the Soul, or such high flown abstractions. But I am afraid that is a particularly brash vice of mine that I can never resist; and, if Dylan could hear me now, he would undoubtedly give me a flip over the head with his fragile hand. Not achieving even a finger-print of impression on such stubborn soil.

However, he got his own back by reading out his poems to me, at prodigious length, just when I was in the middle of some dirty domestic job. Causing a general paralysis of my unresponsively ignorant being. No doubt why I have hardly taken in a word of what he has written: only the froth and foam-breaking-on-the-rocks noise.

In fact, all that seriously bothered Dylan was the arrangement of patterns of words: and which particular word, out of his glorious riches of words, was the most apt. That, and a continuous headache of debts.

The wretched Artist himself is alternatively the lowest worm that ever crawled when no fire is in him: or the loftiest God that ever sang when the fire is going. Who, like the plumber, is more concerned with perfecting the drains which are his department: than the general welfare of the house of Art as a whole. He gets pretty well what he deserves, in the line of spiritual and mercenary remuneration.

If he is unrecognized and gets practically nothing: he must have just enough to live frugally; he is in his proper working element. So, in sheer desperation at the bleakness and barrenness of the prospect before him, he is forced to work to fill up the emptiness. And is therefore richly remunerated by the greater satisfactions of work.

But, as I told you, any frivolous excuse is good enough

for an Artist to avoid work: from hypochondria to hydrophobia. For mocking illness or mocking madness is one of his favourite means of cheating reality, and side-stepping the spreading plague of his dedication.

If he gets fame and a sack of cash he still deserves what he gets. For no Artist can be paid highly enough for the lonely torments he has to go through, and the patience of gestation that he has to endure. But he is no longer in his working element. He is in the wrong element of constant diversions and continual temptations. There is nothing harder for an Artist than to retain his Artistic integrity in the tomb of success. A tomb, nevertheless, which nearly every Artist: whether he admits it or not; naturally wants to get into.

Luckily to Dylan the tomb came late, and he solved the issue of integrity quite simply: whenever in town, and confronted by the easier joys of telling endless stories to buddies in pubs from morning till night, by not working at all until he was back in the penitence of the country.

He had the big advantage too over displaced Artists with their nationalities floating in too much anonymous vacuum: that he worked in a fanatically narrow groove: although there was nothing narrow about the depth and understanding of his feelings. The groove of direct hereditary descent in the land of his birth, which he never in thought, and hardly in body, moved out of. Which handed him his line of approach ready made, and his poems already matured inside him. Which gave him the snail's eye view of a blade of grass: thus imparting to his work his concentrated intensity.

So he never suffered from the usual doubts as to what his craft should be, or what form it should take. From the minute he saw daylight: he had no choice but to write.

His only preoccupations were concerned with the elimination of the fascination of playing too many complex games with overcharged words. With how to make his honey-laden swarm of obscurely buzzing bees more approachable. With how to clarify his clotted exotic images. With how to achieve the courageously simple immortal line: in the tradition of the great poets.

For he always insisted that he was not a great poet: but a great minor one.

But even a poet as selfless, in the human sense, as he was: giving out thoughtlessly and abundantly, from his precious store at the hidden roots of creative life, in a surplus bubbling of words . . . has to be, if he is going to put his words in a final mould eventually, perforce an egotist.

And, if it is true that Dylan is not the greatest of poets: which I don't believe for a second; it is the pity that he was not egotist enough, and his overdose of humanity, that are responsible. A humanity that extended to his own weakness: that permitted him a humane killing.

So need I repeat, fly from the dilemma of the unhappiness of poets, who must choose between being good people, or good poets.

An Artist, don't forget, can never wholly love another person; because he has got to love his craft more. Although, as far as that goes, I don't suppose anybody wholly loves another person. But at least a commoner, having less to lose, can make a better bluff of it. Though even he reserves the major part for himself in order to survive.

I am afraid I am a bit old-fashioned in my views of starving Art in a garret, and consumptive Artists on an iron bedstead at the last lap; for there is a fashion nowadays to dress up the Artist as a gentleman; but that does not change his organically ungentlemanly Artistic instincts: if he has any. Although it is hard for me to believe in the genuineness of this fashionable dog's dinner, this posing dish of fish: having experienced only the powerfully odorous, hairy, scraggy pack of mongrel curs that slink along the gutters of Soho on a sunny afternoon.

However, nobody can accuse us of not being selfish egotists by nature: though perhaps women have got to be more subtle under that sacrificing-their-all stunt. And there is no danger of our selfless soul stuff: that we love to dabble in but not to drown in; interfering with what we propose to do.

We are both also serious and suffering people by nature; in spite of appearing to the uninitiated incurably frivolous at times. But it takes a serious person to be extremely frivolous, for they have a fever for frivolity as a contrasting relief from their seriousness. The naturally frivolous and shallow are more inclined to cultivate pretensions of profundity.

So we do our poor utmost to kill the innate selfishness in both of us. You through your sweet Jesus love; me, through the buffetings to the ground, the steady felling and reducing that time takes care of.

Time heals all wounds, so say the pain hedgers. Omitting to add that it is never too late: even under the crisp hardened cowpat of winter age; to receive a fresh smarting wound. Cutting deeper into the previous cut for all its previous cutting. Ripping off the crusty scabs of the old wound.

But I am convinced that some people suffer more acutely; have a greater capacity for suffering than others. It is this capacity of peeled awareness of all the little agonizing stings under the bland surface of animate and inanimate things: unnoticed by the conforming herd; that causes the hackneyed Artistic sensibility. A sensibility which it is much more comfortable to be without; but which, there is no getting away from it, we possess: if nothing else.

I am not so presumptuous as to assert that my widowed grief was greater than that of many other widows who suddenly lost a loved husband. But my brawl of indignant refusal to accept it was assertively louder: I fear I was never one to suffer in silence; it was a blind fury that strove, with every weapon of defence, to combat the deadness of death. Unfortunately I had never learned, through the church, the deadly lesson of resignation to unnecessary death's foul stupidity. That makes the bearing of grief not easy: but quietly, resignedly easier.

For me it was a crashing anticlimax of steaming emotions. That culminated, in the final stop-gap, in letting off their maddened steam in that morass of confusion and ignorance: that was my book.

A book that now makes me so ashamed that I can never look at it again. Not so much shame of its content: for anything can be said, however awful, if it is said well enough; but shame of its frightful, untidy, messy muck of writing. Which it is impossible even for me to unravel, or make head or tail of.

Obviously written: as some dear old friend of mine observed; when I was drunk. This is not quite true, for it was very difficult then to separate the drunkenness of my mind from the increased drunkenness of drink. There was plenty of both, one on top of the other. With superimposed howling intoxication to spare.

The reason why I speak of the horribly painful subject of the book at all: which after this I shall never speak of again; and the reason why I am writing this prodigiously lengthy letter to you: is to redeem if possible its bad impression on you children. By trying to explain better, and write better, even if I repeat myself, what my feelings really are.

I think I can write better: at least understandably now. But it is always a most laborious task for me, not being born to the job. And writing is the worst job of all, for unlike the other plastic Arts that can get away with much more ambiguity, it betrays immediately the quality, or lack of quality, of the writer. Whose most secret faults are relentlessly laid bare, glaring up at him out of the page, in condemnatory evidence of his undisguised insufficiency.

Answer: try to suppress this mania for putting down everything that is in your head; which is a special weakness of the print-mad English who feel positively undressed without a bit of print to bury their noses in.

Just leave these effervescent bubbles in your head; and, with luck, they will evaporate in superficialities. If they don't: they may be dubiously worth conserving. Look outward, not inward. You may not be so wise by so doing, but you will be happier.

After this orgy of confession, I don't intend to be pontifically serious any more; but to be strictly and seriously frivolous; and to concentrate on the feminine Arts only from now on, the dedicated trivialities. So that you are rigorously prepared for the rigours of entering the beautiful world of the rich.

II

We will ignore for the time being the problem of our overworked souls. There is too much soul about, anyhow: stopping ambitious people climbing to the top. The soul has not got to live permanently under a stone, like a bloated beetle in the dark. That is the Christian method of keeping uppish people down. It can do with a bit of comfort too sometimes, and won't stifle altogether in plush hangings. It is always available when wanted; and can be shaken out, like a moth-eaten fur coat from the bottom of a trunk in the attic; when the draughts of conscience and guilt get too biting.

Besides, we can't get far away from the naggings of the soul: we can only temporarily asphyxiate it. Because it is a monstrous nagging aunt in all of us, that catches up with us sooner or later.

But in the meantime I shall attempt to asphyxiate it by the potent spells of love and sex. Which are inevitably the foremost interests of every young budding girl; and the first stumbling steps in your education towards hardboiled sophistication.

The primary importance is to be able to differentiate clearly between the two. For they are two distinct processes which: though they should function together according to the Educational Book; rarely if ever do. There is love multiplied by sex; but much more rarely sex multiplied by love. So you must learn to instantly spot which is the passing thing and which is the lasting thing. To never be infatuated by sex into mistaking it for love.

Sex is the nice orange juice that makes the nasty castor oil of love go down. Having got it down, the writhing pains in the bowels of love follow; and a nauseating sickness, closely resembling Asian flu, for sheer abject prostration. So love, made palatable by sex, is a painful enchantment that gets viciously kicked in the teeth more and more often as it advances towards extinction. And a love that can remain intact, without the masquerading peacock of sex: through kicking time; is the rarest of miracles.

Love is when the ugly disfigurements about its object become lovable as well. Sex is when the ugly disfigurements about its object are temporarily forgotten: and sneered at in retrospect.

A lover is a perverse pest who is always pestering when not desired; but never pestering when desired. And he is invariably the wrong lover.

He is a gaping yawn of desire when cruelly absent; but, at his sudden prosaic presence, desire surprisingly quickly peters out.

In no time at all the nausea of waiting is wiped away, and the stuffed up cooing doves fretting to be rid of each other again.

So that they can re-experience the ecstatic pain of the separation; with the anticipation of the both foreign and familiar, joy of the reunion.

For a rediscovery of a lover: because the intimacies have already been savoured, and are now being savoured again with a distant difference; is more intriguing, more fulfilling: than the terror of a fresh, most likely bungling, discovery.

But, since love is absolutely without morals, it thrives on doubt, darkness, and lying deceptions. Whereas in clean, above board, padded security: it perceptibly wilts with the tedium of it.

One can take love to the correct trough of convention, but one cannot make it drink. Nor can one stop it drinking from its chosen trough of disreputability.

It is so perverse that it secretly prefers what is low and forbidden to what is honest and allowed.

Jealousy is the lifelong noose hanging about the neck of love.

The dirty blackmail of jealousy is the hardest of all sins to cast out: except in the unlikely case of a Saint in whom jealous love has no part; but it is nevertheless an essential concomitant of love. Without which love is a passionless ghost of love: too tame and tepid to be worth its possession.

For the pulsing organ of love is predominantly possession.

Any love between humans: as apart from the Saintly love; that condones infidelity; with no possessive spasms of jealousy; is a contradiction of the act of aggression that love is goaded to make.

When a once love is as dead as a coffin nail, it is enough to give it the merest tweek of jealousy: for the whole tugging tussle to start up all over again. When, without that extra tweek, it would have petered out ages ago: from its excess of deadliness. Which does not say much for the staying powers of an untweeked love. So it is a case of tweeking a dead love, till it chokes in its own manufactured juice. But at least it lasts longer that way: if not for ever.

So the mutual assassinations that love inevitably entails can, by no stretch of wishfulfilling imagination, be called a remotely civilized pastime.

As for that roaming-in-the-gloaming sex, it merely keeps the world going round in eddying down whirlpools of disillusion and abandonment.

Sex divorced from love is the thief of personal dignity. For however hard you squeeze shut your eyes in Irish style: offering the bestial indignity up to all the constellations in Heaven; it is still not a pretty sight.

Children should be seen and not heard. Sex should neither be seen nor heard. Certainly not talked about afterwards; and it would be a mighty saving to the human race in wasted energy, lost resources, and unthinking indulgence making more unwanted bastards: if it was not done. Cupboard love applies much more nearly to sex, which professionally offers itself in the dim recesses of concealment, in order to obtain material profit. But, like the prohibition of booze, the more disapprovingly the cupboard door is locked on the prostitution of sex: the more rodently will it gnaw its way out through the panels.

For the necessity for it can no more be obliterated than can the necessity for booze. Both are a relieving of the tension of unstoppable continuity: in an explosion of forgetfulness.

Since nobody can deny that sex is all animal: man notwithstanding simultaneously aims to evolve, and succeeds in evolving: into less and less of an animal. So how can all animal be harmoniously related to less and less animal any longer.

A stiff, print-ingrained, paper crackling University Professor, for instance: be harmoniously related to the rearing bull straddling his passive cow concubine.

But then of course he usually gets a cardboard woman to match him; so there is precious little provocation to rearing up on top of her ridged backbone.

There is nothing wrong with the pure animal alone; and there is nothing wrong with the pure Professor alone; but it is when they are frolicsomely joined together that the performance becomes grotesque.

Not only grotesque; but just another of bloody nature's

jokes in bad taste of ludicrous mistiming. Timing in sex, like timing in a dance routine, is the factor that counts, that makes all the difference between a shoddy performance and a slick one. When it is in time it is slick; when it is out of time it is fatal. But how often is it in time. Whatever comes in time. Whoever comes in time. And whenever does anybody come together. The whole history of sex is a disgraceful pigsty of mistiming.

The final twist in the screw of sex is that: while with animals-of-the-land primitives it is so simple and automatic an action that they never think about it again till the next time; with neurotics of the town adults it has evolved into such a complex business that they never cease to be preoccupied by the problem.

Hence their need to go to Freud to help solve their sexual difficulties. Which, as they progress farther away from primitive sex, become increasingly concerned with obtaining at a distance erotic images: to dig into vibration their mummified private parts.

In other words, the more they fornicate, the less they think about it; and the less they fornicate, the more they think about it, and interminably discuss it.

So it would seem reasonable to fornicate and finish with it.

However, no such easy solution is allowed to you; since, whatever happens, we must preserve your precious virginity. Which, though signifying so physically little, signifies so smugly much to the vain male victor of it.

Virginity is a particularly sacred asset to the Latin. For no self-respecting Latin would dream of marrying a girl already contaminated by the ravages of rivals. As repulsive to him as a half-eaten plate of leftover coagulating spaghetti, which it would be an insult for his driven-snow pole to touch.

Equally, if the virgin's dowry is short of a pillow-case,

she will be sent packing, in very short shrift, home to Mother.

But virginity has its mystical value too in other parts of the Oriental world. So it is safer to keep the gold chastity belt relentlessly buckled on; till our Saviour with the golden key descends, from his magic carpet, to unbuckle it.

So we will now leave the cockfight to the kill of sex. Which is responsible for more vulnerable scars in its bleeding trail: than any other variations of the devil's rampant seductions.

And therefore proceed: with our preparations in correct deportment: with the more delicate Art of conversation.

It consists above all: especially for a fragile female who must never forget her social fragility; in not hogging the conversation. But in sitting tight, keeping quiet, and listening intently to her neighbour's brilliant contributions. Or, at any rate, she must look as though she thought them brilliant. With preferably her mind switched off for the most effectively rapt expression . . . With her eyes neither gimleted too grimly into his, nor wandering too far away on a private pilgrimage of delicious fancy. If her mouth must be opened at all, which is doubtful; she may gently part her lips in a smile of winning approval. Not to be confused with a fixed horse-grin ineradicably ingrained from ear to ear on her paralysed face. She may make sweet soft murmurations of agreement; and every so often, but not too often, with timely reservations, let out a ringing peal of appreciative laughter. Which, however, must vaguely fit in with the context of his hilarity.

For the less self-assured listener it is always safe to flatter and praise: though within terminable limits; for there are no limits to the receiver's benign capacity for sucking up self adulation.

So, if she is meticulous never to say what she really

thinks: for that is disastrous unless she is so exceptionally skilled as to be able to make the unpalatable palatable; and merely repeatedly corroborates what her male partner says: if she is never intensely serious about anything; or she will be lacking in finesse: never moralizes; for that is the worst of not-done coarseness: and, most of all, is never intellectual: for that will shock her companion into impenetrable silence; then, and then only, will she acquire a reputation for penetrating insight, and remarkable conversational gifts.

Devoted as I am to the anonymous subject of the weather: to the changes of climate that are a reflective mirror of our own moods and temper; it does not follow that in every country it has the same absorbing interest that it has for the sky-frightened Northerners. Who, rather than be embarrassed by even mentioning their personal passions: fling all their poetic vehemence into singing the contrasts of the weather.

In places where there is a long unbroken stretch of monotonous blue sky, with an invariably grinning sun burning on a posh playground, the sun-surfeited Southerners don't understand our passionate relationship with the seasons. Which to us are the rhythmical counterpart of the cycles of our seasoning beings. Nor do they realize that we are missing: like dogs when they scrabble and tear at grass; the sharp greens, the blowing clouds, the bathing of our dried-up spirit in torrents of pouring down: into its parched crevices: beneficially feeding rain. To them so trivial a subject is merely an unimaginative stop-gap.

So make certain to reserve your romantic waxing on the weather for the stark, cold-blooded Northerner, who is the only true Romantic. To be a true romantic entails possessing no sense of reality: romance being a fabrication of the mind to cloak the excess flesh of the sentiments.

And make equally certain never to impose upon the unromantic hot-blooded Southerner, with such irrelevances to his pressing appetites. Whose chief hypochondriac, saving his liver anxiety, is to creep away from the blinding light; and hide behind shutters to sleep and forget, for a digestive siesta: the killing-his-virility afternoon.

As he tosses and turns in sensual evoking sleep; so we, refusing to give in to our baser natures, as we choose to call them: toss and turn the contrasting climates of our minds: to futile exhaustion. But it would do us a lot more building-up good if we too could only learn to relax the body in sleep and forgetfulness. Instead of being forever stirring and whipping up the weary weathers of the temperament. Which grows fretful in the heat and craves tranquillity. As the Southerner innately knows from so far back that he does not need to think about it any more.

While we are killing ourselves introvertedly thinking about everything we do; they are calming themselves extrovertedly doing everything by parrot ritual. Pretty Pollys in a preordained hothouse of undisturbed forced fattening up.

Though I know it is very difficult for someone as aggressive and inquisitive as you, I want you to try very hard to emulate these repetitive Pretty Pollys. So passively more serene than us in their ancient cages of constricted behaviour.

Within these rigid bars they are permitted all kinds of nice feminine diversions; which I shall now help you to perform to the best of my and your ability.

For a start there is the Art of Dancing: which is the primitive urge to move as the music orders. To forget oneself enough to be spontaneous: and to remember oneself enough to preserve the decencies. To both be the slave of the music's rhythm and the master in control of

the rhythmical situation. It is a fluctuating, but balanced, play between the personality of the dancer and the supremacy of the music.

But the dancer should always: while never losing his head, the long continuous line of the movement, or the muted beat of the time; give the music, voluntarily, its supremacy over him. Its galloping head: while he delicately holds the reins.

Never break off short by force of his personal will, in unfinished staccato jerks: out of self-consciousness or impatience; the winding thread that binds the music together in a compact reel. For the effect will be discordantly wrong and visually unsatisfactory. Whereas it should always seem easily inevitable, deeply fulfilling.

He should never hurry the music: far better to deliberately drag it if he feels so inclined. Or be fearful of its prolonged slowness. For if the music is adequate so will the dancer be in conjunction with it. So he must let the reel unwind of its own volition, in its own musical time; and simply follow what it tells him. Not what he invents in opposition to it.

It is very similar to the intricate play of lovemaking: each giving and taking experimentally from the other, then gradually surrendering to the mastery of love. But, between ourselves, incomparably better. For there are no belittling human emotions to interfere with the final enormous satisfaction of working together in perfect accord.

Such an accord is sadly rare to achieve because the most inspired dancing is done alone; is a solitary union of flesh and spirit in an impersonal void.

When there is a partner there is, besides the consciousness of him, the peril of his interpretation clashing with yours. There is also the double distraction that an audience magnetically creates: removing the complete spontaneity of the dancer.

As for that static ballroom mockery of dancing: of a couple of swooning codfish clasped together in a hazy trance; it is nothing but an excuse for an opportunity of mutual masturbation.

Although, I need hardly say that our upright compatriots: rotating at arm's length with distaste to the imperious ticking of an imminent alarm clock; are not guilty of this unprepossessing habit.

The best dancing to my mind goes progressively backwards. From the unspontaneous brain in the ascendant peak of civilization: back to the spontaneous beginning of the original earth thumpers. Who: because dancing radically shoots from the earth and not the brain; are still, through all their complicated developments, the best of all dancers. When this original thump of the earth is lost: as in the intellectually devised distortions, massacring the music, typical of the German schools; so is the shooting-up root of dancing lost.

For me no brain-fabricated dances can compare, for sheer leaping pleasure: and pleasure after all should be the predominant element in dancing; with the handed down, traditional, gradually evolved, individually native dances of the people. Which are a direct representation of its people's colour, character, race.

What is more beautiful, more subtle, more sinuous, more mysteriously significant; than the Indian dancing. With those seductively curved upward hands, those deliciously dismembered heads on pillar stalks jerking from side to side above an immobile trunk. With jingling of dragonfly bodies, and square padding feet sounding on the boards. But people like us who are neither civilized nor primitive: aware but uneducated, shall we say; should be very wary of emulating the native spring. Or we will merely appear incongruously foolish.

So perhaps it is wiser for us to stick to the domestic

Arts: such as cooking; although for such useless decadents: though I can scarcely call you a fully-fledged decadent, merely a natural-born house slut; cooking is of an infinitely more insoluble complexity.

The Art of Cooking unfortunately, as far as I can gather: is to be born to cook. To fling haphazard, casually unmeasured fistfuls of witch doctor's ingredients into an alarming array of constantly sizzling aromatic pots. While superstitiously looking the other way and simultaneously carrying on a bright tittle-tattling of observations: off the cooking point; to the nervously apprehensive observer, who has nonetheless not observed a pinch. Then rapidly turning out, with light as butterfly's fingers, on an infinitesimal cleared space of the confusingly cluttered table; a mysterious series of appetizing dishes. Each one more surprisingly succulent than the last. All prepared with no visible signs, cooked incognito, and served by an unseen sleight of hand: with an unerring sense of lightning timing.

That is why I suspect, quite rightly, whenever one of these lucky cooks in the blood: with invisible dandelion clocks blowing off the minutes internally and a book of reference only across their dead bodies; gaily says to me: easy as pie to whip it up together in a couple of seconds; that I shall be in a chaos of a kitchen for a good quadruple of plodding hours: of bilious nightmares. And, for all the pedantically calculating labour I put in of deck-clearing, of pan-laying-out-ready: scrupulously tidying up as I go; there are no gratifyingly better results afterwards. On the contrary, my solitary sweated brew comes oozing slowly out in a sticky pummelled lump of solid stodge.

So, except for penitential purposes in uncritical private, that is the reason why I try to avoid domestic work as much as possible; and stick to bone broths that last a week: if one does not turn blue in the meantime. But one can get immune to saucepan poisoning, like anything else.

For those poor inefficient untrained women, like ourselves, who do not previously possess a natural domestic aptitude, it becomes an urgent necessity to learn some other trade instead. For, if the house is such a shameful burden of our inefficiency, we must have an alternative occupation to fill the threat of emptiness.

So what about a spot of dainty, ladylike dressmaking to while away the empty hours: treading water till the waves break over us.

I am very keen myself on the idea of a knitting machine; which I feel would be more suited to my moronic comprehension of technical skills, and less taxing in my senile years. But I think I will put by that ultimate soothing soporific for a wee bit later on. When the last struggle to stop drowning has itself drowned.

But the Art of Dressmaking is not so simple or soothing as all that. Between threading a needle and raving insanity is the smallest eye in creation.

The sewing on of buttons is another crafty manoeuvre to precipitate one's departure for the already threatening bin. Each button being just one more downward stepping stone towards that imminent destination.

That abominable invention the zip fastener, is only used for the case hardened who have failed to respond to the extreme provocation of needles and buttons. For the capriciously teething zip can always be relied upon to get irredeemably stuck on the most awkward occasions. Most likely in the Ladies' or Gentlemen's room. Proving however an even more deplorable predicament for the Gentlemen: who go furiously flying over the borders of gentlemanly control.

Where, once irresponsibly over the border, they are tucked into the downy fold of snow-muffled lunacy; among their own dressmakers-gone-berserk kind. Who are put to such cretin tasks as weaving the future shrouds, or pressing the dismal winding sheets of the late departed.

And they soon forget all about the fashionable mutilations of the fitting room: perpetrated by themselves on the wandering sheep so rash as to enter their spider web cells; so demented as to entrust their figure's beatification into so crabbed sadistic hands: lusting for vengeance.

Vengeance for the injustice that they must do the luxurious mutilations of beauty, instead of having them luxuriously done to them. That they must always be sad and drab in the background, while she: the snake's grandmother; stalks out. Crippled on stilts, tottering in breathless compression, but fashionably triumphant.

So is it surprising that they spurt their extra venom of envy on the privileged client, as a finishing-off hiss; and congratulate themselves that she looks a wealth more absurd triumphantly stalking out: than she did humbly creeping in.

For, make no mistake, in the commerce of beauty, there exists a very deep loathing: an inbred mistrust under the smiles and the compliments; between the vendors of it and its purchasers. Which, at any moment, its sensitive purchaser feels, may burst out, make a grab at her and tread her under rebellious feet. So that the enslaved for so long vendor will thereby promote herself at last to the coveted place of patronage. Where she feels she covetously belongs: with the roles of condescension reversed.

But it is a misplaced persecution on her part to inflict upon the unfortunate purchaser who is not too sure of herself anyhow: probably suffering from a sense of abject inferiority. Who feels already that the vendors are so incomparably more glamorous than her cowed self. In an unassailable position of superiority: for her to model her ideas upon.

It is no great wonder then, with the five caterwauling rages: femininity, vanity, age, class and cash; vieing and clawing at cross purposes against each other in the beauty racket; that some of its weaker cats are scratched and mauled to carcases by the wayside. The wonder is that any are left: still hissing and spitting their feline rivalry on the tiles.

A thing of beauty is neither necessarily a joy: it is much more likely to be a Siberian bore for the holder and the beholder of it, who must both live up to the public responsibility it entails. Nor still less is it: if it is made of flesh and blood; for ever.

To live on minus the beauty that was everything, and now is nothing, is surely more demoralizing than never to have possessed the beauty at all. And therefore, in self defence, to possess something more durable: that does not collapse, like a pricked bladder, at the losing of looks.

Glamour very soon turns to languor. That's where the boredom sets in: when a hallucination dies that has never lived of its own making. Only in the delusion of the beholder who sticks his own transforming eyes into his hallucinatory ideal. Until the eyes of his delusion go dim on him, and his ideal shrinks to normal size. He takes it for granted that his beautiful vessel of delusions is felicitously empty; and so, fair play: ninety-nine times out of a hundred; it is. But he obviously prefers his vessel empty; because then he can fill it up with all the nonsensical fabrications that he sees fit.

The modern tendency to fill up the vessel first with premature learning puts him right off his initiatory stroke. For his vanity demands that he shall be the one to initiate her into the mysteries. Not that he should be humiliated by being initiated by the vessel. So, if the vessel is subtle, she will fake innocence, conceal any disruptive signs of plaguy erudition; and display only a beautiful vacuous pond of pure-as-a-lily submersion for him.

This act of mocking ignorance: when they are not missing a parenthesis of the flirtation; of weak womanly dependence on the fascinating male: is a super speciality of the Latins. And it is impossible to tell whether there is a frog in the pond, or not.

III

I trust I have proved to you that to be a raving beauty is not everything. Which is just as well as you are not precisely that. But a mere passing gratification that, when it disappears, leaves the once beauty-holder more bereft than had they never held it.

So it is much wiser and more rewarding to stock up a rich larder of inner beauty to draw upon when needed in thin times. Which, one can but trust, will shine through in the end and victoriously wipe out the superficial fleshpots.

Nevertheless, we must not entirely ignore the superficial adornment of the fleshy exterior; for it houses the shining out illumination inside. Especially at your stage of teen-age attraction, when you have not yet hooked the fish; but are still artificially baiting the hook. As the open window to this illumination, the freshness of the flesh acts as a reflection of it. Therefore its fastidious care is of first importance.

Although I think the visual sense is vastly overestimated: to the exclusion of the other equally craving senses of smell, hearing, touch, and penetration of an image; yet it is the preliminary point of contact, and has its trifling importance as the first attraction to the predatory eye.

But just bear in mind the over-surfeiting of the visual sense on holiday, for instance. Which causes a profound, if unadmitted tedium; and a dissatisfaction of the profounder senses.

So, although it is not enough to look pretty; yet it is very nice to look pretty. But nicer still to have a deeper prettiness inside as well.

Therefore I suggest that we begin at the top with the Art of Hairdressing. In the same chamber of horrors street; and with the same prevailing tendency to tear to rags the last remaining vanity: as the Art of Dressmaking. But, since the all-seeing head is at stake, deserving all to itself: a head-shrinking chapter of lamentation.

First Act, in the massacre of nature's crowning glory, is the summoning up of sufficient courage to step over the threshold of the terrifying establishment: into a warm engulfment of a cross between a turkish bath and a harem. Or rather, a harem wallowing in a turkish bath. For there are languidly perspiring women lolling all over the place; with a perfumed steam of incensed clouds rising oppressively above them.

Second Act is the shrewdly appraising sneer up and down from the Sheik proprietor of the joint. In order to establish, with unfailing exactitude, the precise age, class, and even more relevantly: bank account of the cringing client. Judging by the look of pained disparagement that overcasts his haughty features: his deductions are not favourable.

Third Act is the inevitable punitive wait: as in all such prosperous snob institutions whose leading aim is the debunking of the individual's prestige. For the express purpose of weeding out the undesirable from the desirable elements. Without which sending-to-the-bottom-of-the-class penance, the procedure would be altogether too pleasantly easy.

Fourth Act is the client in disgrace being led: in full contemptuous view of the chosen, voluptuously disporting wantons; to a looking-glass. And being made to sit pitilessly in front of it: glaring into her own bull enraged eyes. Which seek blindly, wildly for an escape from the ignominous trap. But there is none: for she is dumb, her voice has gone; hence-forward she is incapable of protesting any more. So she impotently glares, and tries not to glare in vain, at her hypnotized reflection.

From now on her head-shrinking tribe are free to perform whatever their perverted fancy whimsically fancies.

Fifth Act is a swarm of lesser satellites hovering round her: not so much like moths around the flame as morons around the freak. Not doing anything remotely connected with the business in hair, but just coming to have a lingering peer: at the thing the cat brought in. Out of sheer rude curiosity. The thing in confusion wonders whether she should break into the fascinated circle, with a croaking comment or two of forced politeness; but her nerve fails her. So they just keep on standing dispassionately gazing: in a static trance of candid astonishment. Giving an occasional navvy tweek at her bush-of-gorse hair. As much as to ask: what strange material is this.

Sixth Act is a sudden galvanization into action, with no apparent co-operation between them, of the maniac animated staff. Her head is abruptly snapped back, and deftly wedged into a viced washing-machine. First ice-cold, then scalding-hot water, is squirted over her skinning skull. Then, with the same airily uncaring nonchalance, a scrambling of eggs lather is beaten up, and prodded at with fork thrusting fingers: always into the identical sore spot. Studiously avoiding, so it seems to her added vexation, the untouched dry regions round the grubby edges. When it comes to rinsing off the lather: it is obviously a superfluous action: to judge by the measly teacup of water they toss indifferently down her neck.

However, as she discovers later to her bitter cost: this is definitely the pleasantest part of the operation.

Seventh Act is the dragging up of her prostrate corpse, by the rat-tailed top of its head, with a permanently cricked-back neck. Whereupon her head is given the briskest of casually flicking rubs with a grey soiled table napkin. Then, with a minute, clogged with old hair, pricking toothed comb for removing lice, they begin to impatiently tear at the tangled tufts; to furiously tug at the drooping ropes of the sad remnants of her bedraggled hair.

Eighth Act is the sticking out of the thin spikes of her hair round her smarting head, like an almost bald Strewel Peter. At this diplomatic point she is heartlessly abandoned to contemplate her ludicrous image: clowning her again in the looking-glass. And to build up fresh, sinking through the chair, fears: of a passing flame in the street happening upon her in her sorry condition. While her gossiping tormentors go in search of a sharp razor. Then, having dug a rusty one out of the bottom of a drawerful of hairy camouflages, they proceed to scrape it down the spikes of her hair: as though it were a saw playing on the wet strings of a very ancient fiddle. As opposed to a fiddle bow on a vibrating saw: as is usually done. The excruciating scraping vibrates in her defenceless ears; while the spikes get less and less long; and she panics: even less . . . Till she resembles a rough-mown lawn, with the weeds still toughly protruding in it.

Ninth Act is the arrival of the wheeled machinery of hair-setting contraptions; and she is graciously handed on her knee a box of frightening pins and clips to hand up to the setter at the propitious moment. The ends of the thinned-out spikes on top are then viciously twisted round jabbing down cotton reel rollers. And all the little straggly bits left over stabbed into her tender under-flesh: as though she were a naughty child being such a maddening nuisance; with the implements she tremulously offers, one by one, to her cross castigators.

Bristling now with their porcupine devices, she is then securely netted: in a hideous pale blue nylon net, which is pulled down well over the furrowed forehead and tightly tied in a dainty bow under the bulging chin.

In her present state of abject reduction, she speechlessly regrets her comparatively attractive Strewel Peter days. But, before she can stray into an escaping world of blessed fantasy, two pink plastic ears stuffed with wads of cotton wool are clamped over her own burning ones. And finally, the whole monster head is roughly shoved inside a roaring cylindrical drying bomb. Where it gets steadily hotter and hotter. Till: if it is not turned down, which they hate to do; she is left to be calmly blown up.

Tenth Act is the roaring heat inside the bomb becoming so breathlessly asphyxiating that it overcomes her silent shame; and she is forced, in spite of her terror of the other women's suavely watching scorn, to scream for help. Without however hearing herself, the pig-sticking screech of her own disembodied voice, for the whirling din within. Eventually, drawn by her frantic waving and flapping, a supercilious minion strolls over and switches down the death-oven by one degree.

Just as she is beginning to breathe a little more easily: though the sweat is still pouring freely down her scarlet face; and look around and notice, with malignant curses in her heart, that the suave Orientals have not even changed colour; and lie back in voluptuous alabaster repose: with abnormal children, instead of breaking up the furniture, reclining likewise at their feet; a slim sinuous creature, immaculate in every crisp detail, minces towards her, and sweetly offers, with a mouthful of nectarines, to do her nails. If the blushing client was embarrassed before: she is trebly embarrassed now. Especially if she has no nails and is sitting tight on her cannibal hands. So, goaded by her sense of self preservation, she brushes the creature aside in a cursory manner, with a too high shrill, or too low mutter of, 'Not *today* thank you'. As though she had only had them done yesterday: or ever had them done before, for that matter.

Eleventh Act is the extraction of the monster head, some unconscious hours later; considerably shrunken as crackling roast pork. Though her dripping face in contrast is enormously swollen.

Once again she is seated at her old enemy, the looking-glass; once again the sunken eyes in the succulent meat peer out piteously at her. And once again the cream of dandified Eunuchs of the Harem: though she reflects detachedly he is probably a happy father of seven children; smarms up to her, swinging his ample hips with eloquent delight.

Once the armoury has been removed from her head by his acolytes, he starts to masterfully brush out, with a hard bristled brush: the burned-up fuzz of pig bristles on the joint.

He brushes with professional artistic strokes; standing back every now and then with his bladder-of-lard head dreamily on one side, the better to envisage the dramatic impact of his handiwork. Then he suddenly surges forward again: all a poetic wobble of inspiration; and makes an inspired dive at it; to coax a couple of coy curls over her crinkling-with-consternation brow.

A gentle persuasion here with delicately picking fingers; a wee bit more puffing up there with a light caress of moulding strokes; and at last he seems nearly satisfied with the final effect. But what great artist is ever really satisfied: as he critically circulates, lost in rapt admiration of his built-up beehive construction.

Twelfth Act is a handglass being proffered to the equally lost client: in amazed admiration of her fabulous creator. But, for the useless life of her, she can't imagine at what angle she should hold it in order to see the back of her head. Which she knows, from hearsay, she ought to do; but which is the ultimate thing in the world that she wants to do.

After a ghastly contortionist glimpse of her unfamiliar 'back' which she prefers to ignore, she is showered with a cast-iron wave-setting lotion, knocking her down with its tarty smell.

So gone are all her secret hopes of ripping the beehive to straw stalks with a giant rake at the first opportunity: for no comb will ever go through it again.

In the meantime she tries desperately: when they are not looking for a second; to give a quick powdering over the glistening pink marble of her face. To identify with a trembling lipstick her disappeared-into-the-marble lips. To tousle into a semblance of natural hair the stubborn construction. But gives up the entire beacon edifice as beyond destruction.

Thirteenth Act is the now utterly shattered client tottering to her feet; collecting in a fearful hurry all her miscellaneous props; snatching carelessly for her moth-eaten coat; stuffing all the money she can immediately find into all the multitudinous outstretched hands in sight: tipping at random exorbitantly, for what has she got to lose; making a stumbling bolt for the door; and falling into smashing reality again. After her long dark internment.

Her only fixed obsession remaining: to get out and go drown herself with all possible speed. Not in water, either.

She had no objection to being made unrecognizable from her humdrum home self: on the contrary, that was her original romantic ambition; but not unrecognizably worse: maliciously parodied. For her film-star vision of herself had been very different from their morbid interpretation of it. And to pay through the soul, as well as the nose for it: was piling on the insults too prolifically.

As she flies down the brightly smiling street, clutching her fairy-doll head, to black extinction: she reflects with embittered irony on her bosom pal's commiserating words: 'Why don't you go to *relax* in the Hairdresser's, dear. It is so good for the morale. And one comes out feeling quite another person: indeed one does; perfectly wonderful.' Perfectly horrorful would be nearer the Purgatory mark of it.

I have omitted, in my punctiliously correct account of the Art of Hairdressing, the extra prolonged and complicated pantomime of first: the discoloration of the natural hair. And second: the recoloration of the discolored hair in an artificial colour. Because I was afraid it would overload my already loaded-with-agonies account to the toppling over point of incredibility: not to mention tedium.

However, I should just like to warn here any brave pioneers still interested in the damage or authenticity of these precarious operations: who are weighing in the balance of decoy improvement the advisability of this chameleon metamorphosis: that they can never be absolutely sure what colour they will, at the terrifying finale, gregariously blossom out into.

That, having come in for example, yellow and grey striped tiger; and intending to be metamorphosized into burnished honey-coated lion: they may quite feasibly come out as slab dead lustreless mole.

So don't you either, dear, be taken in by the Art of Hairdressing's double-headed glorious bluff. Nor be inveigled into thinking that nobody need these days be as flat dishwater plain as nature intended them to be. For, by contrast with the sudden unfitting shocking artificiality, the face: unless it is as blooming as an Irish rose; is inclined to appear as un-prepossessing as a wizened monkey's: who for laughs has donned a theatrical wig.

Notwithstanding that it is one of the primary tidy groomings: curbing nature's horse-hair exuberance in a compact top knot; that the Art of Elegance is ruined without.

The Art of Elegance is another of the Latin specialities, because they are born and bred: money or no money; to the sensual tradition of being always elegantly pleasing to the wandering male eye: that expects nothing less than elegant perfection. In ungarnished words, a correctly conventional combination of garments of quality with matching appurtenances: for each proper occasion. A suitable education to live up to his manly conceits, but never to hinder his undeniable supremacy; and an underlying slavishness of womanly seduction. Amazingly enough, even the very reduced manage to present, by miraculous wangles: this enticing travesty of perfection.

Besides which: the usually moneyed, elbow-and-knee angled Northerners have not a hope in sensuality of competing. Since they are untrained in giving so much time; and such unquestioning devotion to their embellishment. Rightly or wrongly, they believe that there are more important things in life. With the neurotic result that there is discord in the home. They tend to develop into masculine emancipated conflicts: at their most virulent in America. Torn between the physical laws of women: and the male laws of hard ambition. With their sex at a tangent: at a random loss. Obscurely undecided as to what is their eventual, true destination. But neither can emancipation be escaped: once it has reared its Cyclop-eyed head. For it both sees too much, and not enough: to retreat, in content, again.

I am all for a bit of artificiality myself; which is basically what elegance is: trying to pass it off as a natural gift of God. For nature is very rarely so perfect, that it cannot be improved upon. My opinion of nature: especially where its slovenly mistimed management of women is concerned; being mud-bottom low. But the artificiality practised on the lump of clay must be not only an embellishment: but an accentuation of what is already there. For, it is often more the case, that a disfiguring article is clamped onto the clay: for the mere sake of fashion; with no relation to her deformed personality.

Personally, there is a limit to what I am prepared to pay for the price of elegance. A limit which becomes: as the years crawl crankily on, like an out-of-date train; progressively narrower. Whereas to the truly elegant woman there is no lazy limit. Elegance for her is not a means to an end: for capturing appreciative attention in the tyrannical world of the painted surface; but an end in its everyday self. Without which she would feel as denuded as a plucked chicken.

Not only to acquire, but to sustain elegance under every cold circumstance; to be its acclaimed mistress: which is the extent of her confined dream; she must spend a rigid lifetime of rigorous discipline. A regular taxing routine of sacrifice and abasement of the flesh. Not less spirit-consuming than that of a dedicated Carmelite. Similarly, unless she is fortified by a staunch and blazing faith in her vocation, she will fall into disreputable ways. Permit herself off moments of letting down her rioting mob of back hair; of putting up, for a swollen expansion, her corn-throbbing feet.

The nail-studded wooden hardness of the bed she must lie on, makes me comfort myself that her mentality must needs be made of the same wooden texture, to attain her singleness of narrow desire. But I fear I belong to that hopeless breed of common people who put on elegance for Sunday Best, a wedding or a funeral: or such some momentous occasion; and hang it in the wardrobe for the rest of the proletarian week. Who love to lavishly spend, ostentatiously dress up to splash their extravagance all over town. Then forget all about it, and retire spent, to hibernate again in old-fashioned inelegance: till the next great spending day.

But you too, I fear, have inherited my extravagant tendencies to deck myself up in every flashy eye-catching garishness at the same time; instead of restraining yourself to the one simple, cunningly cut, neutral-coloured, inconspicuous tube of basic elegance. Deadly dull of course but fashionably right: which is the Holy symbol. So we must try to restrain our flowery effusions, our native predilection for layers of rainbow striped variety: if we intend to sneak on our bellies into the Temple of Elegance.

Apart from the innumerable rites and rituals of her trade, I ask myself in bafflement: what is the elegant woman free to do in privacy. When not on full dress parade before the ever vigilant Sergeant-Major: lodged on constant duty in her private look-out tower, always on the alert to castigate her for invisible faults, or invisible breaches of good taste.

She may not read: beyond desultorily flicking through the glossy pages of a moron woman's magazine, awkwardly extended in a flimsy shivering négligé on a chaise-longue, with a cup of camomile tea beside her; for any intellectual concentration causes unsightly lines and crow's feet wrinkles.

Nor may she have any stimulants whatever of a pepping-up nature: for they will only let her down afterwards with a sagging bump; with fatal black shadows under her needle-sharp eyes. So that all the normal exuberances of the fun of life are automatically barred from her.

If she loves too violently she will all too soon become a worn-out dishrag with the strain of her anguished passion.

If she loves at all, even with a mild sentimental leaning towards, there will still be giving-away signs of betrayal: of a too strenuous humanity to be in accord with her essential cold detachment.

Better to be on the safe inhuman side: for her isolated peace that passeth all understanding; and keep off love altogether. For love is not a solicitous friend to elegance: which demands all the attention for itself.

If she eats too avidly to fill up the aching yawn that lack of love leaves gaping, she gallops to blasphemous fat. For only a Latin woman, whose elegance is not painstakingly pumped into her, but is as taken for granted as her religion; who can turn a remnant into a raving creation; is capable of so artfully handling her fat, as to knead it into a triumphantly rising dough of elegance. Her secret is: that she does not attempt to squeeze it under false compression: so that it pops out somewhere else, inevitably in the wrong place, in an ugly escaping roll; but expansively makes much eyefully more of it. Makes it the delightful point of focus of magnetic attention.

Even their pregnant women announce with thrusting-it-forward, eye-focusing pride: their treasure trove of pregnancy.

Whereas the poor inhibited Northerners: in their square boxes of flat denial of the boarded-in fat; by denying its spreading volume, merely succeed in stressing it with ungainly shapelessness.

If she drinks or drugs, the hangovering results: which are principally the poison in the body causing the poisoning of the mind, which together contrive to poison the passive elegance of her looks; are too well known to the participators in them to be worth depressingly enlarging upon more.

In cruel fact, she can practise no excesses of whatsoever denomination: even Mystical. For too much kneeling rubs a raw patch in both her smooth skirt and sheer stockings; while the intensity of her religious fervour will make her disastrously forget the sacred preservation of her attire; and her anointed skin will tighten and pucker up unbecomingly in the furrows of prayer. All excesses will lead her faster to her most feared, middle-age spreading, threat of 'letting herself go'. Which she must never: on doom of dowdiness; let herself gradually spread into.

The Black Maria of the cinema and the homely huddle of the television are absolutely Out: for nobody is looking at her. That is the demanding tyranny of her Art: that she demands to be the dazzling: while appearing not to dazzle; centre of attraction.

Sport is far too strenuous and exhausting; and sporting outfits, to be brutally frank, not usually flattering to a refined, unnaturally bouncing up and down woman. Except for that impractical relic of the past: a lady's riding habit for a side saddle; which appears so graceful sweeping down when the horse is standing still. But I have never yet discovered what happens when it takes a jump. The rider remains seated, it seems, by pure feminine suction; against all the laws of gravity.

There is categorically nothing: I have carefully worked it out; that she can do that is interesting: while still remaining elegant.

At the theatre she is seen, of course; but then the theatre is not really seen any more: by the fashionable set. She may dance afterwards in a punctiliously restrained manner: at an exclusive rendezvous. Excluding everything but the restrictions of good taste. She may also go to cocktail or dinner parties. But, since she can neither drink, nor eat her fill: and talks only in polite conventional phrases: these cannot be called precisely interesting. But can any of these activities be called interesting?

Then there is, to be sure, the universal boon as a brain activity of a sort to the mentally deficient: the social habit of killing time by playing cards. Which, while giving gratifying food, of a calculating kind, for thought: actually stops individual thinking completely. Is as useful a brain luller as a sleeping pill.

So, it seems to me, with such a burden of dutiful dullness on her valiant shoulders: with no participation in anything vital: she has a distinctly thin time. That she is destined to be left on the high and dry shelf of china ornamentation: much to be admired; but more to be pitied.

Nevertheless since you must pass through this hard school of elegance too, if we are to attain our wealthy matrimonial intentions for you to save the family fortunes: even if you decide to drop it later like a cast-off tail; here are some few delicate hints towards its attainment. Towards attaining the leopard skin that disguises, with its changing spots: your growling identity.

First you must learn to always appear beautifully comfortable; in acute discomfort. For there is no such assuagement as comfortable elegance: even if some lying exploiters of it blackmail you into believing there is. Take the puffing and tugging on, squeezing elastic, steel-hooked prison of the bust, bum and belly: foundation garments for a start. Then the breakneck, pin-heeled, toe-pinching, stepping on eggs shoes: to be getting on with. Both unavoidable essentials of elegance.

Not only comfortable in discomfort; but also glowing with a mellow warmth when freezing to death. For to be adequately clothed for the varying blasts of the climate, is a contradiction of the perfectly svelte, never bulky, line of elegance; which can only be achieved by being half-naked. No cosy bundling for shivering you in woolly cardigans, or lamb's-wool lined snow boots; both of which are plebeianly inelegant. The less you put on, the better your line will be. So you must be prepared to suffer icy sacrifices for the sake of your slim line.

This painful predicament makes the bearing of elegance doubly difficult in a cold country in the winter. It explains more sharply why the blue-goose-skinned Northerners fail to compete with the coffee-and-cream-skinned Southerners in a hothouse. Voluptuously uncoiling like tropical snakes under glass.

And why: though they can attain a long, stiff, flat elegance of a pedigree greyhound quality; they can never attain the statuesque, rounded, polished antique mahogany elegance of the old South.

While giving assiduous attention beforehand to every smallest pernickety detail of your ensemble, you must appear afterwards, to the public critic, to be distantly absent. Utterly indifferent to it. As though it had somehow, heaven knows how, got itself together by the merest fluke of chance: regardless of your distracted indifference. As though the colour scheme subtly matched itself up in your absence, all unbeknownst to you. For you, obviously, would not dream of spending weeks of premeditated planning and meticulous balancing of shape, shades, and price. Would not dream: no. Only would.

Finicky patience in private, and lofty unconcern in public: are the two opposite poles you must constantly aim at. Significant concentration on the minimum: the tiny precious additional decoration; and ruthless casting off of the maximum: a suffocation of over-opulent furs or a battery of searchlight jewellery.

You must be able to wear a cheap rag that cost a song, with so undefinable an air of rightness that, to the onlookers, it must obviously: because of its very unpretentiousness; have cost the earth.

You must be able to wear a flamboyant absurdity that cost the earth, with so nonchalant a disregard of its exorbitant cost: that it undeniably shows, without vulgarly shouting it. You must show such a casual familiarity with rich materials, such a personal unawareness of their worth; that the company at least is made ignobly aware of your worldly worth.

Withal, a stance so calmly assured as you enter a room; an expression of so serene absorption in far away ecstatic matters; a walk so tranquilly disdainful as you cross it: over the multiple booby traps, the slithering eggs underfoot; past the admiring glances coolly sliding off you, to the doubtful chair awaiting you: where you must adroitly place yourself without appearing to see it, with your dress arranged to magic advantage; that everybody is convinced that you are at perfect elegant ease. Even if you are going through the pins and needles pricking: of the damned amateur. You must convey the impression that you are divinely insouciant of your surroundings; and barely notice the sophisticated entourage thronging around you: so like ordinary home life is it to you. And they must imagine that your almost ingenuous unostentatious simplicity: that you have cultivated at such tightrope complications and expense of tears; is a pure and simple gift of inheritance.

There do exist, strangely enough, such authentic prodigies of graceful elegance; but they are mostly to be found, not in the worldly meeting places; but behind Christ's shutters shutting out the world. Where He prefers to keep them for himself.

What is more elegant after all than the austerity of a nun's habit: repeated in the austerity of her features, unmasked by make-up. With her bird-poised hands emerging from her white cuffs and folding their wings in her black lap. She obtains, from the same abstemious denials of the flesh as the elegant woman, almost the same clear-cut ethereal results. Except that the instigators of their ethereality are diametrically reversed. While the elegant woman wears a pampered face-mask, with a dissatisfied moue attached. The nun grooms the inside the most: the elegant woman the outside. But they must both be groomed daily, inside and out: down to their nethermost toenails.

IV

Having indicated to you a general pattern of Must behaviour; I will now emphasize to you the salient points of Must Not behaviour. But we must consider Cosmopolitan standards, which are severely more insistent on correct etiquette, and fashionable regulations; than the happy-go-lucky appreciation: for any gorgeous gaudiness; of our village standards.

As a trifling beginning: You must not stand stiffly, dolled up in your first starched, sticking out, party dress; as though paralysed by fear of damaging it; with uncooked sausage arms drooping at your inert sides; as though they had nothing expressive to do. With rooted to the ground legs giraffe splayed; or coyly twisting one around the other; like a male comedian imitating a shy little girl who wants to relieve herself.

Nor: to mitigate somewhat your unwieldiness of demeanour with a simulation of purpose; must you clasp a colossally bulging handbag to your taut midriff: fluttering with misgivings; as though about to be struck and robbed.

You must not suddenly jump either: at the preliminary patronizing polite overtures of friendliness; from petrified paralysis to gushing enthusiasm. For enthusiasm is the lowest enemy to bloodless breeding; which you must guard against at all times of high-class celebration. It is in even worse taste than never opening your hermetically sealed mouth at all; which can be passed off as corked up dry wine superiority. Instead of shaming shyness, which it usually unpardonably is.

Neither must you ever give yourself away: in a falsely encouraged confidence; with dreary descriptions of your pedestrian dress-designing talents. Not that such a danger would arise for you: since you possess none. Of your lengthy experimental efforts to run up, in your topsy-turvy snuggery: your gay star spangled costume. Filling you, only too evidently, with overflowing pride. Whilst simultaneously flapping these redundant hands and arms in clown's exaggerated antics. And ignominiously gloating, in a piercing voice: on your wonderful bargain; your wicked indulgence.

Because, in all likelihood, your twitching listener: filled with overflowing boredom and disgust; will be saying flinchingly to himself: yes, my dear, macabrely gay; and morbidly unsuitable to the occasion.

Nor must you ever cram full, into those same ill-fated hands; so logically drop clatteringly all over the floor, more than they can conveniently carry. Not more than two things at once. A glass and a cigarette, for instance, are as much as they can elegantly manage. A titbit to nibble at as well; a large red spotty cotton handkerchief from the Carmarthen market for gale-gusty nose blowings; and a tin of rolling tobacco: are excess baggage.

You must not, at the other extreme, be hypnotized by your feet: that is the treacherous giveaway of the untrained beginner. But firmly believe, however mistakenly, that they will take care of themselves. And, if you have sensibly, if not smartly, put on a pair of solid brogues under the layers of rustling petticoats; they reliably will. But you must scrupulously watch out, when you sit down: not to plant them four square yards apart; like an old rollicking sea captain in a tavern. And make scrupulously sure that your skirt: which nowadays must be a clinging abbreviation; does not wriggle up, of its own capricious volition, to expose your shrinking from the daylight belly-button. While you continue chatting animatedly, blissfully unaware of any untoward circumstances.

So keep a telescopic eye always skinned for any such disasters in your splitting at the seams bolster case. And keep your legs, to be on the safe side, always neatly crossed, and demurely draped.

Modesty and demureness of mien, whether real or feigned, are incomparably more acceptable to the discerning suitor: than gross exhibitions of enjoyment and hearty laughter. Which will only make you unpopular with the disapproving miseries: who will at once term you loud and vulgar.

In whatever society you are, high or low, it is still the beautiful face: both literal and symbolic of masked apathy: the superficial presentation; that is omnipotent.

Record deeply into your memory too, that it is not socially necessary either to automatically say: as I, in the ebullience of my well brought up manners, always did: 'Yes, thank you very much'; whenever you are offered a drink of any alcoholic content. It is possible to say: 'No thank you' without offending. Though wiser, for the sake of communal conviviality, to take an alternative soft drink. Or wiser still, a soft drink disguised as a hard one.

I have warned you enough about: not over-encumbering yourself with too many vital colours massed together at random. For, though each vital colour separately is smashing; when rivalling each other for precedence: they discordantly smash each other.

Or with too many diverse articles of clothing superimposed one on top of the other. For, though each article may be an original treasure in its own right; when put up against another such original treasure: they defiantly cancel each other out.

Or with too many dangling appendages from every beckoning promontory of your anatomy. More distinguished to have none at all; than appear jangling and clanging your alarm bells. Like a straying goat, lost from its flock on the mountains.

It is preferable, if not sensational, to stick to the tastefully merging, softly blending, pastel shades; relieved by that old abominable favourite of refinement, the classic pearl necklace. Dowdily reminiscent of the Royal Family perhaps, but at least subduedly inconspicuous. For, if you can't be a bold flaming cockatoo; you must perforce be a palely iridescent Albino mouse.

The classic tailor-made suit as well: in a good sober material, with quietly retiring appurtenances; is always a dependably conservative uniform to fall back on: when in doubt as to what to properly wear.

You must beware however, that your figure is not too curvaceous in the Latin style: pulled in here, and popping out there, alternately; in order to wear it with the appropriate Northern masculinity.

But to be inconspicuous does not necessarily mean to be elegant: for you can be inconspicuously shabby. It is the matching immaculateness of the whole outfit that is important. But it is a promising beginning; and you can't go far wrong if you are never noticed. It is the twin sister of elegance. It needs but a chic twist of the inconspicuousness; a bright spotlighting at a conspicuous point: to bring it into fashionable notice. To turn the unnoticed into the noteworthy.

To be noteworthy, for an elegant woman, is the plumcake prize for all her paraphernalia of beauty-curbing labours in her night of reconstruction. For her day, you must realize, is but an endurance test; but a trial of resistance; but an acrobatic feat of walking through the scorching fires of temptation unscathed. A self-effacing knack of evaporating in the early evening: as intact as she was in the early morning. To return to her solitary aloof supreme pleasure. Which are; the not-too-hot relaxing essenced bath; the thick wrapping towels, the fragrant scattering of talc. The gently massaged application into her grateful flesh of rich emollient creams, soothing ointments, balmy oils, scented refreshing lotions. Briskly patted on rejuvenating milk, feeding the ravages eggs: astringent lemons closing up the pores again. The descent into the bowels of the earth mud packs. To be luminously cleansed by the penetration of the face into filth: absorbing into itself the human evils. The hair restrainers, the slimming devices, the last warm building up beverage. All to appear tomorrow as impeccable as she was yesterday.

That constant concern for her future: is the essential difference between an elegant and an inelegant woman. The former consistently builds up for tomorrow and suffers today; while the latter thinks only of today, and lets tomorrow take care of itself. Which no doubt accounts for the sudden crumbling of the latter; who finds herself brusquely transported from public talking attention, to private silent anonymity.

At this vacillating stage, in our progress towards female incarceration; I feel I should impress upon you more forcibly the pernicious meaning, and the insidious disintegration, underlying the gathering together of the ulcer Party. With some pertinent suggestions as to how to withstand its ravaging inroads on your strong integrity. Since you are bound, as a coming-out girl, to go to parties: however deadpan grim they are. With modern hoards of half-baked adolescents drooping and dripping their limp lusts all over the contemporary suicidal scene. What feeble-minded wit was it said that glorious, bouncing, aspiring youth: was the prime of life? He must have lived a long time ago; or forgotten what it was like. I personally favour: for obvious sympathetic reasons; the Chinese philosophy that reveres age.

So let's get down to the philosophy of the party: and how best to tackle it.

You must never betray, in your inexperience, that the 'frightful bore' of going to a party: is secretly to you a 'frightful thrill'.

It is not, as you are naïvely apt to imagine, the desperate beginning; or the desperate end of life.

It is, on the contrary, a crass and cruel invention merely to test your social capacity for gruelling survival.

So you must banish at once, from your flightily soaring mind, all absurd illusions of anything so prehistorically dated as enjoyment. Of seeing yourself deliriously swept away; of losing yourself in an intoxicating whirl of brilliant company, scintillating talk, intriguing flirtation.

Of spotting 'Mr. Romantic Right' behind every glass. For the more glasses there are, the more 'Mr. Romantic Rights' there will be. But, when you get him outside, you will very shortly discover to your shocked amazement that, in close segregation, he is not 'Mr. Romantic Right' after all. But has turned back into your old familiar: Mr. Cad-in-the Grass Wrong.

But, if you are so young and so daft: which you undoubtedly are; that you will not learn your chastening lesson; you will surely be buoyantly willing to try again. At the next seductive invitation to a party: fishing in a pisspot for romance.

No, if you wish to master the Art of mastering a party: instead of the party mastering you; you must never romantically gush out your feelings. For sincerity is the damping blanket on the merry edge of humour. It leads to those two yawning pitfalls of provincialism: long-winded heavy earnestness; and, more rural still, petty enumerations of factual domesticities, or geographical landmarks. Both to be avoided like a plague of hymn droning locusts.

But to hold all your opinions, if any: if you have none you will be all the more popular; in light: for lightness is the crowning hypocrisy most to be sought after; disparaging ridicule. Or you, your precious self, will become the butt of their light disparaging ridicule.

The Guest of Honour at the party, you must never forget: is the infamous British scourge of the sense of humour. In which diminishing disguise every subject must be pulled down, distorted, and presented as a verbally spicy morsel of dirt. We hear a lot about the situations our sense of humour has saved. Not so much about those that it has shot down.

No malicious slashings at a defenceless target, are going too far; as long as they raise the scourge-assuaging scream of approval. Of laughing acclaim to the guzzling humour; who feeds on laughs at the expense of negligibly pulped feelings.

Who stamps on fact; ties truth in a knot; makes the flat humped; the straight crooked; and the regular crazily irregular. Anything parodied at all in comical grotesquely exaggerated invention: regardless of the writhing corpses felicitously strewing the floor; to arrive to be the head fabricator of fun in the room. The wizard of word-twisting. To whom all pay unconditional adoring court: no matter what he is, or what he looks like. How foul in every other respect.

And, no matter how strong: tall, dark and handsome; how dumb and enigmatically fascinating his rival may look; put up against the funny man: he is a stone-cold pigeon.

Sex slinks, slithers and slimes, somewhere in the background; but on a pathetically secondary level to humour. And, unless it can be lasciviously humanized into a ribaldly scoffing tale of jolly bawdry, it is definitely not a decent subject. No more than a lecherous indecency done in haste on the back stairs: swilled down swiftly afterwards into shamefaced oblivion. Never to be vulgarly referred to again.

Sex, in any case, is a much safer plaything to leave to bearded rollicking men. For women, if they are so rash as to mention it in a light frivolous vein, will only cheapen themselves in the eyes of the best upright citizens.

So, first and foremost, always remember at all trying times, that you are predominantly a woman. Which above all signifies possessing all the womanly guile and graces that she is made to deceptively practise: by men's blind desire for them.

There are nowadays all too many emancipated women; who all too often do not remember that they are legendarily passive. Who are carried away: to men's sneering disapproval; by the force of their manly utterances. With a thumping punch in the chest of their adversary: to thump home the power of their muscular beliefs.

Neither does sharp wit sit easily on a compliant woman; making her repellently unwomanly. Frighteningly like a shrilly quipping jackdaw dodging in the unreachable treetops.

Being a woman proper means embodying, in the feather-lined nest of your person, a small fragile hatch of couched softness and fledgling sweetness. Which is what true womanliness: God help our rhino hides; still personifies.

Or, if it does not any more, the myth still holds good. For the strength of weakness and defencelessness: backed up by cascades of crocodile tears; are potently still the most irresistible. For they appeal to the same weakness in man.

It means that, even if in reality her yielding shell contains a hard-boiled yolk of mercenary ambition; a pecking chick of shrewd calculation; she must serve up her garnished egg at the table of male delectation: all a-shake and a-tremble with soft-boiled, running-over compliance.

It means that the relevant stress must insistently be on the symbols of femininity: bust, bum, legs, lips. In preference to the charming irrelevancies that trickle and bubble from her deliciously pouting: or incredulously parted alternately; dewily moistened lips.

She may part her lips almost continuously: if it so becomes her best; in an intimate conspiratorial smile. Which, while saying sweet nothing, precisely readable: suggests so much, deep everything, unread.

Or: to vary the ominously gathering monotony; she may recklessly open wide her rosy-spittled, pearly-gleamed mouth: in a cascading scale of bird-twittering delight. Which polished performance, has taken her dark sessions of experimenting: to so ingeniously perfect.

She may then, so suggestively in unison, manipulate the curvaceous assets of her shape: if inadequate, she must contrive to make them additionally adequate; in so consciously an unconscious manner: not a thought in the world of attracting attention; that she is in permanently pleasing: but never pushingly offensive; mobile vision.

Admittedly: this sensual mobilization of the body is a special, superlatively Latin gift again. For they have no ridiculous false shame about being stared at with eyes and tongue slavering out. It is the wine of life to them, without which they are no longer desirable; and therefore defunct women. But it can be acquired, with slogging patience: by a shapely Celt at least. Provided that she has enough corkscrewing body to wriggle ingratiatingly, and wobble provocatively. Jogging up and down, and swinging from side to side; like a trotting pony, on her clamorously clicking hooves.

This freak extraordinary; this weird fabrication of dog's dinnered dish of fished to kill womanhood; with genteel affected, insect-mincing gait: to humour men's odd conception of what a pollen-brushed butterfly woman should resemble: with no relation whatsoever to her original cocoon; must now memorize parrot-wise the ruling Party prohibitions. Which can be summed up broadly as:

Never to contradict, argue, express a bigoted statement, or make a strong dogmatic assertion of any sort, on any conceivable plane: except strictly trivial. To dare to be ponderously serious is precipitously approaching the blue-stocking area.

She may however be permitted a girlish rave: as long as she is genuinely girlish enough to get away with it; over some pin-up singing star of the screen or music boxes. For her foolish, gauche raving will appeal, by contrast, to the knowingly nodding wise elders. Simulating endearing foolishness is an infallible trick of the Party trade; which even the sophisticated woman frequently uses to her ice-breaking advantage. Then cynically directs: to further her own cynical interests.

It is also a useful and most effective form of flattery. Which, by emphasizing the unbridgeable gap between her light, ball-of-fluff head: and the weighty, hairlessly bulging domes confronting her of the impressive guests: causes them to feel sceptically above her; but pleasantly patronizing, kindly condescending: in such a shallow stream of running on rippling chatter.

So they unbend in the melting aura of her muddle-headed banalities: her crushing platitudes. Disport themselves freely before her cuddlesome infantility: rolling on the ground in her conversational clap-trap. And:

unrestrained now by mental rivalry: reduce themselves to frolic, as skittishly, in her foolishness. Having foolishly already swallowed, in one gullible gulp: her elusive dragonfly bobbing bait. Did the fools but know it.

There is a slightly more involved dodge: on the same theme of wide-eyed, open-mouthed vacuousness; to which I am particularly partial myself: since it covers so neatly: my conspicuous-for-its-absence education. That of doing the village idiot act: with such an air of disguised intelligence; that it is arc-light clear to all: by a sprinkling of dropped gems of inadvertent culture; that one is idiotically putting it on. When all the time, of course, that is categorically what one pointedly is: an authentic village idiot, with a scrappy sack of bones and bottles.

One more sugary nice ambiguity too; when uncontainably infuriated by some vilely impossible statement or act, and not wishing to show it too rudely; is what I call the angelic insult. But to produce it effectively one needs the necessary props: round pink, cornflower-eyed, haloed in fair baby curls, mock angelic face; and the gentle drawling, tender tone of voice. So that nobody can quite believe that anything so diabolically unlikely came out of such a pure undoubted angel. That she evidently can't have meant what she said: or that they must have misheard it. But her rubber-bladed carving-them-up knives nevertheless rankle in retrospect: and a distressing element of doubt remains. Doubt that perhaps, after all, Archangel did intend her Arch-fiend insinuations. Causing a fearful consternation in the honey combs of their smug complacency.

So, having got your swarms of stingless hornets and scorpions, stuck, drunk and dazed round your slavish dolt show: don't go and spoil it all: misled by your precarious eminence, and a couple of extra fizzes; by plunging into a sudden blackout of cantankerous yelling indignation. Against all that is wrong with their egotist conditions; their depraved sewers of life; their dandy affectations; their dilettante sins of omission: omission to what? Words fail you, but only temporarily. Then, gathering steam again, fervently exhorting them on: how they ought to live. How, by simply giving away all their burdensome property and possessions; they will earn the inestimable secret of threading their cleansed souls through the almost invisible eye of that minute needle: into Paradise on Earth. And so be as gloriously happy as Saint Francis: with a rock for a pillow and only the birds of the air: as preferable, and cheaper incidentally, than the birds of the street: for company.

No dear, that is definitely not a tactful approach. Or your horrified devotees will instantly disappear, like fur-scorched vermin: in the searing flame of your unpopular fervour. And you will be left preaching your ideals on The Betterment of the Corrupt; to an emptily echoing auditorium.

It is best too, to avoid entirely, tempting as it is: the mention of Death. It is not conducive to lifting the general morale of the party. Except in the sense that the party goers are still alive: in a sense; while the dead indubitably are not. So this tiny difference alone, cheers them up considerably; and adds unwonted zest to their lucky survival.

Nor is unconvivial God the most popular member of the party in his original sinful guilt. So don't go harping on about his tiresome mission: of casting out the swine in all of us. With a piercing gaze round the table at the swinish Heathens: looking shiftily askance. Who have grown fond of their fattened swine; and have no intention of toppling them down the debauchery stained mountainside.

The party is not the propitious place for casting the

oppressive shadow of quiet: contemplation, silence; over the forgetfulness of the proceedings. Over the floating memory of bad things done that ought not to have been done; and good things that ought to have been done: left undone. It only causes an embarrassed terror to take possession; a turning away of the guests to shelve the unsightly blemish to some suitably distant date: in the unknown horror-chest of the future.

When conversing: it is much more comfortingly cosy to stick always to the personal and the particular. Where everybody knows, with responding relief: where they are. But be very attentive never to make your comments too personal; nor too particular. Well divided again with the fleecy lining of wily subterfuge.

Then, when their taut resistance has slackened, a warm exchange of imaginary intimacies: only between our selected selves of course, and the doorpost; can be elaborately constructed to keep the windy spaciousness of the world: small, familiar, and as far away as the cold uncongenial moon.

Gossip and scandal: if you want to gain the magnetized attention of the crowd; are unfailingly gourmandized rich titillators of the appetite. But again you must be most pedantically particular: never to hit upon the physical appearance, combination of attire, or cascading down the falls reputation: of one of your own catty sex. Because, before you know where you are: she will be spitefully hitting back at you, with a vanity-pricked cat-of-nine-tails.

Reverently refer to other women in the room: in terms of unbelievably honeyed sentiment. Even if you loathe their guts, and your words sound blatantly false to your ears. For, through their wishful hearing ears, they will be complacently sucked up: as their unquestionable, justly obvious due. They will go around saying that you are not half so bad as they thought at first: in spite of your unfortunate, putting off exterior. That you reveal a real understanding character underneath.

Don't be backward in coming forward: to lay on dollops of dripping sentimentality: especially to the mellower men who are less realistic. For, provided it refers to themselves, and their sloppy own: they will guzzle it up wholesale. Never even notice the gelatinous lumps of lying in the unctuous mush.

However, make unmistakable that it is their credentials; their photographs; and their life histories: that are being displayed so presumptuously on the mat. Because they won't be a bit interested in yours; and will think contemptuously: Oh God, that ghastly old sentimental line again . . . Instead of the reverse.

When playing on the sentimental blind-spots of a famous, spitted, bearded and deaf sugar-daddy; who jocularly gives you a resounding slap on the bottom: try not to jump bawling in the air with repelled fury. But instead give a breathless gasp of flattered delight: and rub the spot in fun with coaxing squeaks of pleased, invented pain. Whether or not you would have preferred, by far, his handsome son to commit the objectionable affront.

Perhaps now, to polish off my wise party-going counsels; I should give you a guiding introduction to, and a brief summary of, the limited types of people you might conceivably be likely to meet.

V

The Pervert

Because perverts are nearly always cleverer: so logically made to suffer for it; than the average functionally normal person; they are consequently also more sensitive and more responsive. So they make the easiest most amusing company with which to start the evening: and to continue it incidentally. Except that it is a social duty for you to vary the types; and to get into voluble practice for besieging the stodgy stone, dense wood, impenetrable bone walls of the averages.

Because as well they are intimately familiar with all the feminine details of intimate apparel; and the elaborate decorative make-up of the superfluities of her feline seductiveness; they possess, in addition, that extra sympathetic intuition of a woman. But with the brooding, moody, cud-chewing cowhalf of the woman delicately removed. And in its place the sparkling gift of male quickness, and interpretative talent attached.

Nevertheless: if they are roused to bilious envy or jealous displeasure at the perfidy of a love-mate; they become ten times as petty, twenty times as spiteful, and a million times more scarlet-taloned: than any housewife-homely, doing-her-daily-dozen, whore.

The Decadent

Decadents too are excessively good company at a party: since excess is their roaring trade; and the main attraction in their shop of decadence. The only nervous fear of the company is that they will suddenly leap; with no apparent provocation; from being excessively pleasant; to being excessively unpleasant. From gay tipsiness: to excessive drunkenness. From friendly badinage: to excessive pugnaciousness. From polite compliments: to excessive amorousness. Or, without any warning, abruptly retire and be excessively sick all over the best bedroom carpet.

But thankfully, at least there is no fear of them being padlocked into their dumb isolation of self-preservation. Believing they have nothing to lose; they don't mind losing it. They revel in thickly spreading the contagious stench of their decay: as a door opening into a stuffy room of sleep laden, sweat congealed vapours: assails the morning-keen nostrils.

Whereas the primly isolated, stingy life-blood preservers who think they have something to lose, are forever on the lookout to protect the precious hoard of their secreted treasure from marauding pirates.

The incorrigible decadent delights, on the contrary, in his decadence: as a parturating sow rolls obscenely in its own bloody muck.

He not only can't change his state of decadence: which is a hereditary accumulation of ills; but he does not want to lose his licence in disreputably shocking excess.

I ought to know for: among other improper things; I am a proper one.

The Artist

You have already had sufficiently pummelled into you: the utter hopelessness of Artists from every woman's permanent point of view. How, when they go to a party: since bleak barrenness is their natural element in which to work best; they do anything ludicrously unacceptable to destroy the previous intolerably real, seeing too much reality. And incidentally, destroy themselves as people: in the blinding of reality process.

Since they give to their work all that is most vitally stimulating in them: what is left over is, unavoidably often, inarticulately vague.

To a woman: don't be led astray by his fine words of Eternal Faith; he can never give more than his secondary human half. Which: even if it is sincere, good, loving; is inevitably secondary.

Therefore, with all his piled-up drawbacks, since he rarely has money either: for Art never pays enough, and if it does, he can't hold on to it; he should be put away in quarantine: for a rainy day that never comes.

Of all the Artists the musician is usually, for some obscure reason, the most prosaically dull. Never emerging, as a defined individual, out of his own mysterious cave of mathematical music making. Because, I surmise, his material is so prophet ecstatically the opposite: of his grounded self as its instrument.

The painter is usually the slowest, the calmest, the most even-tempered, the best looking; and, I am told, the best lover. Presumably because it is his prerogative to draw the figure in the nude. So automatically, as his further draughtsman's prerogative, he must probingly study the anatomy of his model.

Which makes him also, to my mind, the physically vainest. Although the choice is confusing with so many warring Artist's vanities to choose from. So, as a sad sequence to a bullfrog blowing out of his vanity; he is the densest too. He has even got the impertinence to try to write: which is a contradiction of his visual material. Dipping and diving into his overcrowded coloured ocean, with pretentious density. While very few struggling writers would seriously try to paint.

The writer is usually the ugliest, definitely the most nervous and temperamental, and undoubtedly the most interesting. Because, however pedantically verbose, he does after all use words by profession. Instead of musical notes, paint-brushes, or sculptor's chisels.

He can even be very entertaining when he feels like it, in his own sweet time. Though he is more likely to be so if he is a lesser writer, who expends himself more liberally with compensatory wit. Or, better still, if he is a flopped undeniable failure: who must give all he has of his imaginative fantasy: to justify his failure.

I am convinced that the work of the writer is the hardest: besides which hacking rocks in a concentration camp is child's play. And that: since he is forced to use every squeezed out ounce of his intelligence; he is the most miserable, so sympathetic, devil of the lot.

The Sculptor

The sculptor is the spitting image of the hunks of stone that he sculpts. A hunking great chunk of stone, with a ponderous belly-button in the wrong place by sacred law. With surprised odd-sized peepholes popping out of it haphazard: playing peep-bo pranks with you. In a baffling conspiracy, an insoluble conflict, between the womb dominated pendulous weight of stone; and the sculptor's soaring image. Which point-blank refuses to soar.

As for what the sculptor thinks he is doing: if he thinks at all; only he and posterity know. But, fortunately for baffled Artists, posterity does not show its damning or pedestalling hand: till the player in question has retired from the fray. For, of all enigmatic sphinxes, sculptors are the most enigmatic: of the whole slyly conniving sphinxery.

Then there are the interpretative Artists: such as actors, singers, dancers and musical instrument players; who come into another quite different, snobbish class of precedence one above the other. A relentless class of colossal vanity; of ruthless ambition; and of vicious backbiting envy: among the cliques and clans.

Because, their Art existing only in the present actuality, in the living moment of performance: in the now or never of time; they obviously depend more urgently on their looks, their youth, their health, and their sustaining ability.

So their Art: because they must make an immediate presentation of it in their visible shapes; has a desperate element of dread panic in it. For the day, which they constantly envisage as their final curtain: when they can perform no more. When the body stops; and the spirit goes on ticking without it.

The Guitarist

Take the fascination of the guitarist as a typical example. Will he never realize that he is not, perforce to everybody, the most fascinating creature in the Universe. Will he never understand when his performance is logically over: never know when to stop. For to stop him is synonymous with stopping his Universe; which must logically go on for ever.

Never comprehend when the wilting listener, who prefers the sound of his own voice, is glutted to nausea. Or that his seductively willowing presence, bending forward over the table, mouthing his amorous incantations: is not the most encouraging accompaniment to eating. Making completely impossible concentration on either the food, or his persuasively gleaming eyes and teeth. But such a born exhibitionist cannot conceive of anything so puerile as plain embarrassment; or the shy writhings of introverted people: in his all winning presence.

If only he could be heard in the background distance:

preferably through butter muslin; it would be so restfully preferable. Then somebody else could talk for a change. For not everybody is a happy, lethargic listener to hypnotic noising. Some like their own awful noise best.

Like the amateur handy-man, the interpretative Artist can't bear not to be watched intently all the time: while performing. For him it is an unforgivable insult to his Art: not to be given your intense, undivided attention.

For, when practising his instrument alone, for him it is but a necessary preparatory training. He gets no fulfilling-in-itself satisfaction like the creative Artist. His supreme fulfilling satisfaction is in the response of his audience. The magnetic relationship between his public Art: and his public's responsive vibration to it.

Whereas the creative Artist only gets the applauding or booing of the mob later on: when his Art is already detached from him. And he feels indifferently: apart from the mercenary gains; no longer part of him.

As a possible, presentable boyfriend: I would strongly dissuade you from having anything to do with an interpretative Artist; who is even more unbelievably selfish than a creative one. And that is saying a glutton's mouthful.

The Provincial

The provincial is possibly your best bet: taken as a square leaning block; in the marriage market. In spite of his lukewarm, cabbage-water respectability; his rabid, frothing-at-the-mouth conservatism: with precious all worth-while to conserve; and his devoutly conventional dress and behaviour. But only so long as he is keenly observed by the neighbours: of whom he is petrified pink. By their witches' eyes peering and peeking surreptitiously from behind a lace curtain of an upstairs window.

In spite of his passion for imitation. To be just like

everybody else is the blunt peak of his craven aspirations. His cautious obsessions for solid lasting symbols, like comfortable security; for providently looking ahead insurance. He has a veritable mania for insuring himself, his family, and all his Godly possessions: thereby deluding himself that he has achieved immortality.

In spite of: his adoration for the ordinary. For every ordinary average man's sensible pastimes. Like daily newspapers at the printed barrier of silence breakfast table. Sport, and prayer-intoned sport scores: on the radio, on the television, in the muddy field. No matter where, but without the handy entrenchment of sport, he is too vulnerably at the mercy of the wife's henpecking.

In spite of: his one little forbidden vice of restrained betting: with pinched from the kitty shillings. Creeping up the side of the street, under cover of eating hours, when nobody is around: into the bookie's office to put on his small, but miracle-promising bet. Which might, one never knows: hypothetically might be; but never is: the unique key to escaping riches. That eternally fizzling-out dream of the misled over-optimistic self-deceivers.

In spite of his upright manly duty to escape from shaming domesticity; from a too ignobly homely mother; and from a squawling clan of pestering and badgering children. To quaff down man-sized pints of best bitter beer at the 'Cock and Bull' local: with his identical, pipe-smoking, hearty booming buddies. Downing, with the rising flood of beer, the smelly dregs of his home life.

In spite of his tedious reverence for counting his conscientiously accumulated pile of savings. For minutely pricing each trifling acquisition to his hideous worldly goods. For comparing, in his favour it goes without saying, how much more his glossy objects cost: which to him are not simply glossy objects, but faithful reproductions of his own glossy soul; compared to the trashily cheap ones of those common people next door.

His tedious reverence too for funereal pomp and plush hanging drapes. He is prepared to spend a fortune on a beautiful gilt-coffined, wreath-laden, marble-head-pieced funeral. All for a useless relation that he bullied to death when alive. But truthfully: all to impress the community with his rich lavishness. It never occurs to him that its lavish cost is a trifle redundant. Since the little bag of skin and bones: whose dubious identity is tactfully ignored; is not entirely there. Not present in seeing person: to get an appreciative eyeful of all the fuss and flowers: that never came in its lifetime.

This obvious discrepancy is the abortive drawback to funerals. They should be staged beforehand; so that at least the Corpse of Honour could join in the jubilating celebrations too. They are not staged for the dead, but for the living afterwards.

But what does the narrow Provincial sod know of, or want to know of, the undulating subtleties of death. Of living deaths or dying lives. Of death in life: or life in death. Since he is nothing more: his quarter living self; than death warmed up.

Nevertheless, in spite of all his putting off, prejudicing against him, faults; in spite of his being all posh lavishness on top, and wrinkled sour grapes below; nevertheless, if you get an exceptional Provincial, he will preserve the same inborn sense of sacred esteem for the united family; but he will rebel against all the binding of all the individual taboos. In reverse he will be exceptionally open, individual, free thinking; exuberantly and dangerously generous with his worldly belongings, virile powers, and mental gifts.

The only impending catastrophe is that he will go too riotously to the other, opposite: banknote flinging in all directions; Artistic extreme. Show too great a lack of restraint. In which tragic case he will be a greater dead loss, as a dependable husband: than the unenlightened grooved Provincial. He might even go so far as to become a cracking good Artist: for many of them do; and that would inevitably be the end of wedding bells for you.

The ideal for you would be to get a compromise between the rooted, stuck-in-the-town-gutter, Provincial: and the rebel who tosses his trilby over the slag heaps. Then you would get both the homely comfort and regard for your cosseted keep: plus a stimulating human being. Who thinks when he acts; rather than acting by repeated unthinking habit.

But perhaps we are asking too much; and getting too choosey. Or else, at this analytical rate, you will remain a pining spinster till a taxidermist comes. Which doubtless is the happiest way to be: if not the most acceptable to a girl craving for the fruits of matrimony.

The Gentry

I have already warned you to be wary of the Gentry. Because, apart from anything else, they are quite bluntly, as a general class: too mean to live with. Meanness in marriage is the least tolerable of all the partner nagging, detail niggling faults. Which becomes an increasingly more: molehill into mountainous; fault.

The only really charming Gentry are the fallen Gentry; but with their charm, unhappily, goes their charmless lack of cash. So I fear they are out of our pregnant race for the confinement couch.

It is not only because I happen to be one of the fallen Gentry, that I think them charmingly preferable to the seated Gentry. But it seems evident to me that one who expends too much of his landed property: which is tantamount to saying himself; is bound to fall. Whereas one who holds on to it too tight: for preserving privileged life; is bound to stay seated. Hence meanness is a necessity: for retaining the family seat.

The fallen are invariably more fully and warmly human; because they have both the weakness and the courage to make mistakes. The weakness to fall, and the courage to pick themselves up. Then make the falling mistakes all over again. And so on, in habitual succession; till they have no strength left to make any more variety of mistakes. Although the will to make them: is not lacking.

The seated on the ancestral throne are more fearfully inhuman; because they are too rigidly bound together ever to make mistakes. Too hidebound and limited to experiment in anything new or unknown. So they remain snapped shut in a hard and narrow pocket book of spiritual limitation. Of meanness of spirit; and meanness of pocket.

The Journalist

If I have said anything derogatory about these varying types of people, it has been derogatory only as far as they concern your welfare as life companions. But where Journalists are concerned there is no word so derogatively stinking that it sums up the congested stink of their constipation.

They are as disruptive a menace to the public body: as grating turds in the intestines are to the private body.

They are the scavengers of society who, possessing no guts of their own, tear out the guts of celebrities. They have the sycophantic, false enthusing gush of maiden aunts: who are accustomed to being trampled on doormats. So, with bitterly suppressed bile and rancour in their peanut hearts: they pretend to enjoy surrendering their humbled selves before: paying court too: the shining stars way above them.

When, since their servitude began: low down in their hollowed breasts; they are brimming with pettily spiteful envy. A twisted screw of pettiness and spite is lodged there: biding its screwing time.

Which later on: after the sweet surrendering act; the hypocritical jollying along; the all-pals-together lie; when they write up: the chatty intimate interview; they then viciously vent on their victim of greatness. However, cheaply obnoxious as they are: to be poked at with long sticks as one pokes at a dying viper; they are not a serious worry to a big enough person. For, however lyingly libellous they may be: nobody can seriously hurt the reputation of a Great person. If he is hurt: he is not Great. They can but scratch at his skin with their mice nails.

But it is prudent for you to be fully aware of what a suspect class of undesirable humanity they are; and to be very cautious never to be taken in by their devoted protestations of true friendship. For they are congenitally incapable of true friendship: or true anything else. Except perhaps romanticism, which flourishes on the growth of: no sense of reality. Like a blind mushroom in a damp cellar.

The Coloured People

Like with the Jews: it is a snobbish *Must* nowadays: to love the coloured people. A snobbish *Must* however, that can change overnight: into a snobbish *Must Not*.

So don't you ever dare to be swayed by, or change, with snobbish fashion. Because: whether or not you happen to detest one particular member of the coloured race; it is your Holy responsibility to treat them all with equal consideration: as any other more privileged race.

More than that: because of the foul and filthy persecutions they have been made to suffer: it is no longer permissible to treat them with the same racial carelessness. You must always give them instead an extra indication of your especial appreciative regard; and make your sympathy felt. But beware, as of a rattlesnake, that you never show the remotest trace of condescension.

Or they will spot it at once; and despise you for a pretentiously ignorant oaf. Which, in fact, if you do such an ignorant action, is precisely what you will be. An ignorant oaf with brassy knobs on, who would deserve all their pitying contempt.

Although I am perfectly sure you would never be so insensitive as to behave with so little feeling for other people's feelings.

The trouble is that a lot of stupid people don't even feel: when they are hurting other people's feelings. It is intentionally the last thing in the world they intended to do; and their gross offence has to be painstakingly pointed out to them afterwards. Whereupon they react with shocked amazement, and emphatic denial of ever meaning such an unkind thing: the last thing they would be capable of.

Like the kind ones who shrilly exclaim, with gloating delight: expecting equal gratified delight in return; 'Why, how well you look, my dear, putting on a nice little bit of flesh lately, aren't we? But don't worry, it's only puppy fat': playfully poking and prodding the anything but puppy lumps and bulges.

It is my firm opinion notwithstanding: that these personal tormentors of the body that can't help it; do know: even if only subconsciously, but frequently consciously too; what they are at. And, one infallibly finds on inspection, that the blemish over which they are tormenting one, is, strangely enough: one of their best embellishing points. That they are conscientiously, with cruel kindness, rubbing home the contrast.

In my case, these sadistic people always seem to be deliberately elongating their tapering lily-white hands; with ten-mile-long pointed, shinily-varnished nails, curving up at the ends; under my nose. And gracefully waving them to and fro: as though contemplatively unaware, in an abstract trance, of what they were sadistically doing. Like abstract Hell.

Or saying, with a glutinous smile of melting wonder: ' – but, my dear, you can't possibly be the mother of a twenty-one-year-old boy: I *don't* believe it; when*ever* were you married. *Well*, you certainly carry your years magnificently: how*ever* do you do it. You are so *won*derfully preserved: nobody would ever guess, I *pro*mise you.' Or: 'Why, my dear, it's *absolutely* amazing. What *have* you done? You look *positively* ten years younger! Anybody would think you are well almost: quite a young unmarried girl.' As though I flaming cared, at my abandoned stage of life. Although this little stung tirade certainly suggests that I do.

But there is here the treble insult of one: the suggestion that one could incredibly wish to look younger in the first place. In theory one should be looking all right as one is. Two: that even should one have incredibly wished to look younger: it should not be so self evident. Because that suggests that previously one looked a ravaged wreck. Three: that, even presupposing both these prior suggestions, it is a compliment to be told so. It would be a compliment, on the contrary, for it not to be noticed: so naturally fresh and young, as always, does one look.

Cruel stupidity, and thoughtless tactlessness, are responsible for more penetrating hurts in the tender squirming innards: than any other form of brutal beating punishments of the rhinoceros-skinned exterior parts.

The penetration of a pin as opposed to the bang of a carpet beater.

So don't think, my child, that you are the only one who has suffered these crass indignities; from well-meaning acquaintances. Like an advance of tanks in a flower bed.

For all young people go through these self-conscious torments: only some, put apart, are sensitively worse.

One simply grows to care less: but never, wisely, not to care at all. But perhaps that wisdom too grows; with a year or two more battering down of uncaring age.

The extraordinary phenomenon is: how ardently the old people do care. Even in the worst homeless, soulless institutions for the old; where they are made to feel the shame and uselessness of going on. That they should have decamped a long time ago. How ardently they cling to their tatty remnant of life. Like merrily leg-clicking crickets, cling to their snug holes in the hob of the fireplace.

I suppose because there is so little left of it; and, as it decreases, it becomes increasingly precious. So they must make the most of it; whatever their unlivable circumstances. It is now or never: with a vengeance.

But I don't think anybody really relishes the idea of the black hole. Not even the Christians who, in theory, go whizzing up to Eternal life. For life without a body to put it in can't be much fun. And those who say they are not afraid of the black hole: are either extraordinarily unimaginative or plain liars.

It is the idea of missing something. Of the world having the presumption to go on rotating without his unique sun. That each one for himself, however lowly, can't help being; that is so indigestible.

Since the world is seen only through his unique sunlight: in accordance to how he has lit up his patch of vegetation, through the crack of a door ajar; how can it, disembodied from his rotating light, go on in the dark without him.

It does not strike him that not the whole world: but only his patch of world; has gone into the dark. Which, logically for him, is saying the same thing.

And everybody: though they may long for the oblivion of the dark; is still afraid of the unknown threats of the dark.

Like taking a train to a new unknown threatening destination. Instead of staying securely in one's own known awfulness. The awful comprehended known: against the awful incomprehension of the unknown.

That is the awful snag to suicide too: that stays the hand at the prick of the slitting throat. The fear that one will not be 'there': to witness the distress and consternation on the dismayed faces of the loved ones. What is worse, the more galling fear: that one cannot even be smugly sure that there will be any. Perhaps instead there will be a rejoicing heave of relief. . . . So naturally, to give them such a disgusting satisfaction, is: out of moral principle; out of the question.

Besides death: since one can't go back on it; is too stupidly dead. Which is why faltering would-be suicides change their minds at the decisive: going-over good-bye. With a feeble excuse of virtuous indispensability, leave their deaths to the dissection of the worms. Whose department rot and decay is; and who fatten on corruption.

'A short life and a gay one' is a lot of self-pampering, vain nonsense. For a short life does not, by any fair or foul means, guarantee a gay one. Youth is so self-centred that it sweats and swoons with melancholy. At its restricted incapacity to live on a higher inspiring plane: than that of the stifling restrictions of its incapacitated family.

While gaiety comes with the 'letting go' of disillusioned age. What does age care about the capacity, or incapacity of life any more. Age cares about the miracle of still breathing: which youth takes for granted. Miraculous breathing: so it is gay.

The Pappagallo

Literally and fitly: the parrot. Although you would hardly be likely to meet a Pappagallo at a respectable party. Unless he gate-crashed by wangling graft, which is his specialized trade. Because they normally frequent: since they are a popular product in sensual demand there; the milling-with-tourist beaches abroad, of the numerous summer resorts on the Southern coast.

But, as you will probably be going abroad yourself at some likely time; it is most incumbent that you are minutely prepared in detail for what: insinuating into your company tactics; to anticipate from these professional beach boys.

They are the exact prototypes of the indoor gigolo; with roughly the same plausible approach. An insidiously making up to you means of endearing themselves: to your facile sensibilities.

But practised instead in the visually stripped body: and invisibly stripped soul. Searching for foreign dupes: in the more knobbly-kneed revealing out of doors.

So they are a permanent menace to anybody so oddly perverted as to sincerely wish to be alone. To bask in peace; and cretinously enjoy the sun and sea: for their own beneficial sakes, and healthy content. Who do not wish, with a single particle of their being, for any such passingly empty, dispiritingly futile, adventure. Sapping them, both of their hoarded energy, and their hoarded collection of savings.

But the sole abnormal incongruity that the Pappagallo is vaingloriously: to the point of being locked up among the striding up and down, madly grand Napoleons:

unable to believe: is that he is not the irresistible answer to every matron's prayer. Or that anybody could actually prefer their own company: to his irresistible desirability.

For such a strange aberration of the distorted course of nature, goes offensively against all his preconceived notions. Of tall, rangy, red-skinned, sex-starved blondes; from far-away barbarous places of snow and fog. One and all pitiably lusting after his boiling, purple churning blood. One and all loaded with a wad of crackling Heaven; at his instant, prolific disposal.

He fancies he has but to flash his toothpaste winning, symmetrical row of shining bite; to be timidly beckoned to bound: with the lissom agility of a hotly hunted hare; to their warmly welcoming sides, shuddering with responsive emotion.

That the frightened white rabbit will respond prostrate, to his black, tentacle-twining advance: of ham imitation love.

As a prospective Pappagallo worthy of the job, he needs to possess the following attributes. First of all: extreme, prancing youth. Then a strutting, puffed-out chest, hirsutely coated with gorilla matting. Next narrow, sinuously undulating loins, tightly trapped in bright, private-parts-revealing trunks. Private parts which he is constantly adjusting with a loving hand. Presumably to remind the customer: as though she could possibly forget; of his irrepressible virility.

To continue his list of progressive charms: silken, sun-blackened, sea-drenched limbs; never still, but always in eyecatching performing motion. With always the superbly crowned head of profuse coils of oily, crow's-wing glinting, tousle tempting agitation of hair. Sprouting strongly out of the moronic eyebrows: over the luminous as glass eyes. Straying softly down the robust erect neck. Wandering gently, in downy streaks, down the animal back. And disappearing into the furry nest of folded genitals.

Lastly, a sleek-speaking tongue of shameless, spilling platitudes. That is adept at quickly picking up: like a ravenous ant eater; an impoverished smattering of slick phrases, smart colloquialisms, parroted slang: in all the different, variously pidgined languages. With which to sugar-sprinkle his pawing insinuation into paying intercourse. When understanding nothing intelligible in any language: but that of mercenary commerce.

They have the imaginations of wrinkled black olives; and the avarice of green unripe peppers.

They venerate only two deities. Their mothers: who represent their superstitious fear of, and crawling on their bellies respect for, the Madonna. And money: which represents a divine slice of solid property; everything most ecstatically desirable on earth.

But there is no hope of a doubt: between the mother and the property; of which of these revered properties would be sold for which. If it came to the blackmail pinch of their chameleon consciences.

What profit they make on the beaches: from rich idle hypochondriac hag scare-boys, craving for diversion and new blood at any price; or from wealthy elegant sophisticated queers from bleakly civilized continents: grubbing in the sand for the panther primitive vitality they miss—(for whom the scale of pay is higher, because to male perversion is still attached a Latin ignominy; and a woman, after all is said and done, is still, upside down, recognizably a woman)—goes to feather the future breeding bed for their patiently waiting bride. Patiently hanging in the wardrobe, out of sight: till that gloriously auspicious day.

Till her traditionally yearned for: as the sacred destination of girlhood: lifelong day of mule servitude begins.

Or, God help her, left uncourted and infertile, to serve in disgrace in her own deriding family.

In a hovel overflowing with unstoppably continuous, ragged brats eating her alive.

Working day and night at all the burdensome beastliness of insistent family demands. In a health and heart destroying endless rotation.

Then falling, like a sack of potatoes, into bed; for the fabled exotic, sensual refinements of the marriage union. With her long-past-noticing her Lord, and brutal beating Master: whose every spoilt foible is a divine right. Too tired even to protest against the tyranny of his demanding love: out of an unwanting numbness of time.

With never enough money for the crying necessities; in a frustrating insufficiency; in a lowering deprivation; in a continual anxiety of shrieking strife; in a criminal desperation of worry and want; she becomes, if such a superlative is feasible, even more money-minding; more haggling of it; more grasping of it: than her money misering husband. And precipitously more beautiless; rapidly expanding into a fermenting barrel of secreted tears. With the implacable loss of looks and vitality of constant mothering. Mothering by implacable law: till there is no squeak of an embryo left to mother. Than himself, still unmarred and beautiful, sitting back watching it all; and resignedly shouldering his put-upon father's obligations.

Marriage without the small assuagements: the curtaining of the ugly corners; the sordid concealing embellishments; the magic prince transformations that money brings: soon deteriorates into a cantankerous nagging match of nerve-breaking wills.

A married pair who would love each other peacefully, under happier circumstances; are, by lack of lubricating fuel to make the engine run smoothly, driven to hate each other.

So watch out you never marry a penniless, no-good bum. For: whatever spell of enchantment is cast over your infatuated head temporarily; the marriage is doomed to founder, on the destructive rocks of dirt, dust, and poverty.

Watch out keenly too: that you never get so besotted by the heady potion of burning out your resistance sun; melting and confusing your judgement wine; and the drugging melody of Latin glamour: for glamour, if nothing else, they possess by the truckload: in a sensual atmosphere of unresisting lethargy: all mixed beguilingly in a potent aphrodisiac sauce; as to ever give the smallest flicker of encouragement to one of these pretty Pappagalli pimps.

For they will only skin you: not only of your wage packet. And rape you: not only of your honourable virtue. But, in the demoralizing process, remove every atom of your self-respect. And your name and reputation, should it matter to you, will be dog's excrement. Not only in the eyes of the proper, honest contingent. But in their improper dishonest eyes: at your easy acceptance of them.

Admittedly, it will mean: if you are unaccompanied by a male bodyguard; that your glamorous holiday abroad will have to be spent perforce: in your hotel bedroom. For the only means of escaping persistent molestation: is to leave the beach free to them, as prerogatively their reigning province. With the solitary muffled diversion of peeping through the slats of the Venetian blind: at the fascinatingly vicious goings on, spread before you panoramically on the beach. Which, although a most absorbing occupation: superior to a cinema any day; was not the humiliating fate that you had in mind, when you set out on your long journey: for the thrills of the Continent.

But at least by doing thus, your moral prestige will

remain triumphantly intact; and they will reverently look up to you, as a craftier-than-them escapist: from their woman's sex snapping snares.

Had you been so foolishly fearless as to accept an invitation to the bar, from a hen-cocking Pappagallo: where they stand patiently all night, nursing a Coca-Cola, in cock-crested readiness for a weak fallible prey to cascade into their brass cage: devil a bit you would get in the way of liquid sustenance, unless you paid for it yourself. What is more, you would be expected, as a matter of course, to pay for the regal favour of your Arabian Night of seduction: with a delinquent parasite. For devil a bit more in the world they possess, than the coxcomb they stand up in.

As for myself: I can now wander almost at will where I will abroad, in comparative peace. For in no advanced state of ancient monument: is there complete peace for a woman abroad. With no more fearful trepidations of piercingly persuasive wolf whistles hissed insultingly after me. Yet so perverse is the lower nature of women, that: though I am truly enormously relieved at their blessed absence, and my immunization from such rude attentions; there is still a cheap negligible inkling of regret left in its embers, that sickeningly moans: 'Am I gone so unattractive then now, that I can't even raise the ghost of a wolf whistle any more.'

The perversity of women consists in the impossible to achieve. They don't want the nuisance and indignity of being followed. But they want the followers to want to follow them: without going through the farcically coquettish business of it. Otherwise it signifies that they are not worth following; and there is something wrong with them as women. Of the two alternatives they would generally prefer to be followed and bothered; rather than nobody want to follow them at all. Which accounts for the more womenly women in Latin countries, where they are followed as an obligatory homage to their womanliness.

And the less womenly women in the Anglo-Saxon countries, where they are left in perfect undisturbed peace. Which smells to them suspiciously like rejection of their womanhood.

So it seems only reasonable that they should seek for more appreciation elsewhere: in the Oriental reek of abroad. To reaffirm their womanhood with simpler, more direct, straightforward passions. Pushing physical over hesitating mental.

It is scarcely surprising then, and scarcely their fault, if they end up with a parody of manhood. As husked of his pride of manhood as corn off the cob.

A parody as petty, empty, and degenerate, as the summer bloom of the passing Pappagallo. Passing into Satan-only-knows-what holed hibernations of squirrel nutting winter. Till the next far away, gathering in of the grain summer. Of his tidal influx of tourist livelihood.

Vomit on the tourists as he will, he can't live without them; and when his selling glitter of gems is past: what then for the useless mug: too soft and vitiated for an honest job of donkey work. Too far beneath one who has served the privileged, in his privileged capacity. I never cease to be struck by the contrast between the intoxicating beauty of the Pappagallo's countryside; and the pinched ugliness of their little souls that are impervious to its lifting up influence.

Well, so what is that to me: that's not my lookout. Why must I always stick my long sniffing nose into other people's affairs that don't concern me. It's up to him; he can look after himself far better than I can. As though I had not enough gnawing troubles of my own: of what to do next in nothingness.

There is a difference though, between the drop into nothingness of an enlightened person: as I choose to call us; and the drop of an unenlightened sod from the sod: inescapably back to the sod.

For the enlightened have at least a few stacked in the granary resources to fall back on; and to help fill up the vacuum of sky in the nothingness.

While the unenlightened: having never risen into this taxing the brain area of over-penetrating light; has no distance to drop. So, in the sense of changing levels, he is no worse off than he was before. He unfairly comes off better, than the drop of levels suffered by the enlightened one.

That is why: in the dark abysses of convicted State detention: he also suffers less. Because there is less of him, lit up inside, to suffer.

He goes from his familiar dark: into the same, but unfamiliar, dark.

The suffering one, with his chastisement of light: goes from its partial glow, into the pitchest contrasting darkness.

So it would seem it were more gaining of content, to gain no light at all. Rather than to gain just enough to suffer by.

But simple as it is to kindle a light: once kindled; it is not so simple to extinguish it.

Not many are willing: having once seen the rewarding realities beyond themselves; to put out the light. To go back into cow-stalled, beast bedded-down, dark-stabled: elemental ignorance.

The element that is most important towards the achievement of enlightenment; towards learning to see clearly: the outer world seen through the inner world; is curiosity. Lowly, common curiosity: that is not afraid to poke its vulgar nose where it does not belong.

The unenlightened ignorant are preposterously uncurious; they slothfully, don't want to know how the other half of the world lives. What they think: what they do; because they just don't care enough. They have not the searching imaginations to care.

Curiosity and caring are an implicit part of each other. Caring is the heart that pumps out the blood of curiosity: to go and have a look.

As you know, I am ravaged by an insatiable curiosity: to see into all the places, where we are never allowed to see. So that must prove that I carry a lighted torch of curiosity: that teaches me all that I know. For none of all that I know is out of books. Which, you will probably say, is why I know so little. To which I, with a flash of repartee, will reply: 'Ah, but it is better to know a little well, than a lot badly.'

I am not maligning what is learned in books. Only saying that the removal of oneself: into a detached space of static immobility; does not suit me. Since I am too self-conscious to read with complete absorption of myself.

I prefer tactual learning. Touching, on the quick of the sore nail, of present, mobile life. To toy, to gnaw, to tear: at the living element of pain. Like at a living drumstick.

It is not only the size of the pain that gives it more potency: although its size too has obviously a potent part in it. But the capacity for pain: for the amount that one single human being has the capacity to take in.

As the capacity for love and happiness demonstrated in enclosures of pain.

How well I understand the capricious contradiction of those once pitted in the pit of pain. Who are strangely loath and fearful of being summoned out of it. Fearful that they can no longer live up to the taxing obligations: that the bracing air of happiness entails. So they huddle back into their painfully adjusted angles: in their hiding pit.

As some pained people stick fearfully in their hiding slums: when summoned to better, modern conditions.

VI

The Intellectual

Since the Intellectual is the farthest away manifestation from the primitive; the Pappagallo; and, incidentally me: I am afraid I can't tell you much about him.

Except that I don't think his is a very felicitous state of mind to be in: though I may be wrong there again. Because he is intellectually that himself: a state of mind. A system of thinking; with an incurable vice for analysing all his thoughts. Which prevents any spontaneous eruption of feeling.

It is possible to have a mind built to be an intellectual: without the education to furnish it. But to be a functioning scholar: which it is his business to be; and to function correctly; he depends perforce on having a thorough education. To draw upon for his scholarly work; and in order to come to his just, fully-fledged intellectual stature.

Or, without it, he will be no more than a scaffolding of bare rafters. So, being in this predicament myself, I have an exaggerated respect for his scholarly knowledge.

The result of so much undiluted mind stuffing: on him as a human being; will be a drained dry deficiency of his humanity. And his prospects of personal social attractions will be extremely dubious. Since he is neatly cut off, in his printed paper mansions; from all the human sides of life.

So I don't think we need consider him as a serious

menace to you at the party; and hardly likely to be entering your suitor-seeking orbit: of prospective possibles.

Unless he has: as they sometimes do have; a pathological mania for the contrast of sappy juveniles: to his erection of skull bones. Secretly likes to mingle erotically: his dryness of parched flesh; with your succulence of fruity flesh.

The Dipsomaniac

The Dipsomaniac on the contrary, is understandably: the miserable manifestation that I know most about. If not through his entire complex evolution: through my own conflicting tendencies in that destructive direction.

At a party, he is not a profitable contact for you. Because, after his first, spontaneously genuine advances; your vibrating relationship will be steadily swallowed up: in the vibratingly dominant attractions of the liquor.

He will see you eventually, through a bemusing cloud of dazed enhancement of your image. Which will have no human connection with the real you: champing and chafing under his storm of euphoric rain; and lost in his blindness. Till he precipitately becomes unattainably divided: by a blaring, blurring ocean of drink; from any articulate contact with you.

An invading ocean; which he spends his tortured time slipping in: and nipping out of. Being drowned over by it, and saving himself in the conscience prick of time. Frantically trying in vain, to get to the safe dry bank: so near and yet so far. But always, just on the brink of it: slipping in again; and going under fast. Till he goes under for the last dipsomaniac time.

By the morning: it is an understood tragedy; he will have forgotten all about you. Or perhaps some vague, nostalgic guilt about you haunts him. But he is wreck tortured only by the remorseful agonies of his pitiless hangover. His single intolerable desire: but only those like him will sympathize with his abject illness; to cure, by killing, his hangover. By the very same undermining methods that made it.

For there is this malign curse laid on dipsomaniacs. That they must absolutely have a drink: in order to feel strong enough to stop drinking. And having had that drink: as every helpless dipsomaniac knows; another must absolutely follow ... So there is no end to his yoked martyrdom.

Moderation to him is more impossible to attain than complete abstention. But he is not a bit fond of abstention either.

Having lived on spasmodic nervous kicks: to keep up his staccato pulsing; the flop down into a stagnant puddle afterwards, is too timeless; too permanently going on for monotonous ever. For him ever to be able to permanently resign himself to.

I should be very pleased indeed, if those scoffing hearty fools: who guffaw with superior amusement at his unmanly disgrace; could be made to suffer one-third: for more their heartiness could not survive; of his acute suffering. So that their stupid, heartless pomposity could be taken down for a day visit: to his underground cemetery of shadow-boxing skeletons.

After one glimpse of his condemned isolation block; shared by similarly sentenced prisoners: all under condemnation to premature death; I don't think the hearties would feel quite so cocky as before.

The dipsomaniac, being so near to it; is in constant fear of, and struggle to the death: with death.

His brakeless trend is to go downhill. So that when: by some miraculous effort of will, or preventative circumstance; he manages to penultimately cure himself, and never touch liquor any more; the resulting absent creature:

speechless with an inarticulate sense of loss; makes his despairingly trying to cheer him up friends feel: that it would have been kinder after all to have let him gone on fatally: but deliriously downhill.

Since the creature is but an unwound up robot; and out of the world already. So it is too late to try to stuff him up again: with reanimating juice in a faulty engine.

The Fanatic

The Fanatic is an individual who fanatically believes in what he says: even when it is logically proved wrong. Even when it is a scientific fallacy. He is not interested in objective truth. Only in his own fanatical truth.

But a dash of violent clashing fanaticism: if it does not overrule the personality to the extent of blind mania; is a most useful and colourful driving asset to the personality.

Particularly helpful to dealers in specialized work. To achieve the necessary concentration in one specialized direction. To work through a concentrating tunnel of specialization: that any specialized work requires. With the same fanaticism of the snail, blinking out of its house-shelled concentration: at just the one little slimy patch on the wall; where it fanatically intends to ascend.

For, without the initial prejudice: which is the fire stoker of fanaticism; the personality is too uniformly even. Too flat with acceptance of all the sheep braying creeds. Too widely diffused: absorbing in every direction unanimously; to be a stimulating influence. To be a driver instead of a passenger.

But, as far as the fanatic influences you: I should be very chary of accepting his prejudicial, steam-rollered-down pronouncements; which, after a short subjection to them: will become a dogmatically repeated pain in the neck.

So bear with the less flashy types; and resign yourself to the normally dumb, more reliable: fornicating by unprejudiced procedure; unfanatical ram.

Freaks and Eccentrics

Since I am not quite clear as to the difference between these two aberrations on the gliding liner of society: I must lump them together under the same definition.

Truthfully I believe that nearly everybody: if not everybody; is a freak and an eccentric. But that most, cowardly choose to mask their freakishness and eccentricity: in outward bluffing uniformity. Only a few courageously behave as they feel; and frankly proclaim it: if not flaunt it. And, because they don't care what society thinks: they are consequently a whole lot nicer and happier. They are also the free-est people; with the least false conceptions attached.

However sharply the cocoons may ridicule the wriggling out striped caterpillars: the caterpillars still get the last laugh on the cocoons. By their happy indifference to it. And in thinking the cocoons: in their stuffed shirt cocoonment; infinitely more ridiculous.

All the same: they are not suitable company for those who wish to make an impression in society. So: while enjoying their freedom from formal snobbery in private; try to cautiously avoid getting branded as one yourself.

For such freakish and eccentric indulgences are not permitted to a well-brought-up young lady. Only with ridiculous and rich age is it permitted to behave freakishly and eccentrically. Also: if the name is important enough, to make a famous impression thereby.

But then, to the famous every indulgence, in freakish eccentricity, is permitted; and labelled unsurpassable distinction.

The Neurotic

There is the genuine and the feigning neurotic. But, it is a misleading universal heading: for a vast percentage of people who have not the rare distinction of being officially labelled Neurotics. As the proud official cases have.

Labelled official: by those who attempt to cure them. Who are, disastrously often, more neurotic themselves than their own doubting patients. Doubting not only themselves: but their doubtful healer.

There is no black and white dividing line between a Neurotic and a non-Neurotic: whatever the opposite of one may be called. For there is no such thing either as a standard unchanging normal being.

Least of all a natural from the land; where, in illiterate villages flourish unchecked every twisted tree root growth of unavowed: therefore more prolific; human deformation. Clamping down on the disproportioned mind: to make mincemeat of it.

He is a negative misfit: so dissatisfied with his refusal to fit in; that he must steal the fitting-in satisfactions of the odious, but envied, positives.

He is immovably held up in his action stops of negation. That stop his free performance of the instinctive elementary action.

So: from his frustration of insufficiency; he must justify his existence by performing in a noticeable way. That differs discordantly from all the other smooth harmonious ways.

By crashing discord he therefore obtains, at least, notice. For he craves, above all, notice and attention. Which are his neurotic system of exploitation. His neurotic craftiness in getting his own back: by the blackmail of commanding pity.

So you: who like us all; have surely got a malleable share of his neurotic craftiness: must be judicious not to use it too flagrantly as a blackmailing tool. Or, in times of serious crisis, when it is urgently needed to wring the withers with irresistible pity; its potency will be annulled by over-exploitation.

You will be confronted instead by an unyielding hurdle of weariness. Wearied to detestation by your eternal neurotic moans and plaints.

The surprising thing about genuine Neurotics, is the surprising places where they are to be found. Not so much, as might be expected, in disreputable Bohemian sewers: where there is no thwarting malady of too much bottling up of reserves: too much unbottling is the trouble there. Though there are plenty of feigning Neurotics in Bohemia: throwing their compensations for talent around. Or in working class congestions of sardined incest. Which does no evident harm, beyond moral disapproval. The social stigma attached to it.

But respectably tucked away, out of impertinent eyeing, in Suburban fastnesses of shamed suppression. Where, in such closely protected retreat, the unspeakable genuine Neurotics thrive. Burgeon unrecorded; revolt mutely: in padlocked chains of prosperity; against their unloved segregation.

Till, when turned unmentionably Neurotic: not decent to be seen by shocked visitors; they are discreetly packed away in expensive, glossing-over-the-disgrace clinics. Where they are left in central-heated, sense-doping comfort. Soothing the consciences of their banishing angels, who say reassuringly to one another: 'Oh, but she will be much happier in there; so well looked after; with all the help that modern medicine can now give her. There have been such wonderful advances in that: long pause; field.' Then, a little nervously: 'She may even improve, and get better; you never know. And won't it be nice if she gets fit enough to come home again. However, these nervous upsets take a long time to cure: and we must be patient. Plenty of rest is what she needs.'

Whereupon she is then forgotten: as completely as though she had never been; by her less revealingly neurotic relations. So she continues to rot, unsung, her rotten life. Trickling: like a leaking tap; down the drain.

For, to be a genuine Neurotic is a luxury that the poor can't afford. Or else: if they allow themselves to go so far in luxurious demonstration of it; they are banished into Public Wards; containing the dregs of mental demoralization. A fate which they are most alert to avoid.

But to be a Neurotic alone: without a sobbing and lamenting audience; is no sadistic fun either. To get the full rich, spicy herbaceous, flavour out of it; he must compulsorily make himself an intolerable burden: to some poor, doting, over-credulous slob. So that he can wield: to their fullest slavish satisfaction; his neurotic weapons of tyranny.

There is nearly always a mother, who is the obvious slave to her neurotic offspring.

By which time she is probably an owl-screeching Neurotic herself. Wielding back at them, in double measure, her tenacious, leeching on to them, tentacles: of a mother's blackmailing love.

' – After all I have done for you, my darlings: all the bitter sacrifices through the long growing years; that you thoughtlessly, as ungrateful babes and sucklings will, took for granted . . . I gave you everything I had: the best years of my life; and not the smallest little word of thanks have I ever had from you in return. I ask only for the smallest little word . . . is it too much to ask? How could you treat me so?

'Leave me all on my own: now that you have no more use for me; to fend for myself. Cast off and abandoned: like a soiled sanitary towel; in a cold and lonely world.

Left loveless, with nobody to love. Is there not one among you: oh my beloved sons and daughters; who will comfort and look after their failing mother: in her weak old age?

'Have you no gratitude in your stony hearts: oh, you unnatural traitors of your one and only mother. For, be warned, I beseech you, for your own sakes: there is only one mother in a lifetime, this side of Heaven, and you won't get another.

'You will live, my cruel dears, to regret this day of betrayal yet. And, when you, yourselves in your turn, my daughters become mothers: you will understand what it is to be a mother . . . And how you, in the callousness of youth, broke the heart of: and killed your own poor mother.'

In such slobbering vein: slobbering on; and self-pityingly on; interminably . . . Soaking up, with indescribable relish, her shifty offspring's inescapable subjection to her; the mother asserts her predatory claims.

Only by discarding her children before they discard her: the wise mother knows; will there be a remote chance of their voluntarily visiting her later. Of their even being quite fond of the old trout.

But: though there may be a warring tangle of Neurotics in a family; one of them, at least, will have to give way; and retire from the surplus of competition. Be willing to play the scapegoat to the others. Or else all their petulant complaints of: paralytic spasms; mysterious aches; and confounding strokes; will fall on the deaf ears of the rest of the jealous suicidals.

Too many Neurotics in rivalry: not only confusingly spoil; but murderously poison the broth.

There is this danger too attached to feigning Neurotics: that if they go on feigning too long: they become, before they know where they are: genuine Neurotics.

Who make you pay, not only in hard resounding cash, but pay extra: through the pierced nose of the soul.

I had most particularly not wished to touch on the delicate subject of this sensitively flourishing group of ever multiplying: and no wonder; Psycho Pedlars. For already, I feel with hurt, sufficient derisive fun: to fill a garbage pulping dump; has been made at their vulnerable expense.

After all they are only honest working boys, plying their trade, like anybody else . . . Doing their poor best: well, not so poor perhaps.

Because their profits seem to be so inordinately out of proportion: to the unenlightened in such subtle differences; to the profits of anybody else: that does not mean that they are quacks or profiteers.

Not anybody can continuously sit on their expanding bums all day: owl-nodding at the life stories laid out, like red carpets, for them to trample on. They have got to be qualified to do it.

There is an elaborate Art behind the studied movements: each one with its separate significance; of the Psycho Pedlar. Years of intricate study have gone into the perfecting of his slick and polished technique. As exacting, in its muscular controls and contortions; as the most austere school of classical ballet.

The same lengthy training: from tender pubescence, is necessary to master his ordeal of staying statue still, like destiny on a rock: for consecutive paid periods of his valuable time.

The same rigid discipline is imperative to achieve his faultless timing, in assuming the correct posture of listening inclination: at the preliminary dribbles of information that hesitate and falter on the threshold of articulation.

The same superhuman restraint is demanded in retaining: through the gradually swelling floods of emotion; his aloof manner. His murmuring accompaniment of lofty condescension.

The same steel will-power is commanded in sustaining: as the turbulence of floods mounts ominously; his strictly distant deportment.

The same dedicated patience in private: alone in front of the mirror; is needed to manipulate and coax his recalcitrant features: when the flooding tension threatens to break over him; into a sublimated, out of this soaking world, expression.

The same scrupulosity, like the priest's, in practising: to quietly subdue the now obstreperous floods; to curtly order back the surging waves of gushing on, and on, and on . . . Interminable trash of talk; the economical use of words.

And, at the crisis of hysteria; at the traumatic, vomited-up fag end; as the guinea-pig, in a frantic access of fixation transference, manually transfers, its compulsive obsessive tenacity, upon his shrinking back substitute figure; he must be constantly on the alert, on his fleet running toes. Must instantly improvise, and deftly execute: the eel-twisting trick of shaking off the guinea pig's misplaced embraces. With such consummate tact; and such devastating finesse: that the guinea pig is not even aware that it is being shaken off.

Then, pulling the ripped strings of present reality rapidly together again, he hastily wipes the floor with its past complexes.

Next, with a punctilious regard for punctuality; and a professional chucker-out's force of character; he gallantly, but domineeringly, shows it the door.

Until it comes crawling back, at the next appointment, for another dowsing in its own buried floods: from its buried flood dominator.

So you see, you must never show your ignorance, by making light of, or underestimating the profound omnipotence of the Psycho Pedlar: who knows perfectly well what he is doing, if nobody else does.

You should make a boast, as I do, of always being open, and responsive, to new progressive ideas. As open, in credulity: as a gaping village idiot. For it is more enriching to suck in too much: even if it is a mouthful of flies that has to be spat out afterwards; than not to suck in anything at all.

The only really unforgivable sin to a Psycho Pedlar: is uneventfulness of experience. Having nothing awful enough to tell: for his jaded appetite. Which, I suppose, is understandable, since he has got to listen to the everlasting scratching record of jammed experience. With the needle jammed in the same, constantly repeated groove. Or as the tongue jammed in the same constantly throbbing tooth.

But: although sympathizing with his tedious predicament I should like to offer him some practical advice: for disinterring the wireworm root of the trouble. Not to dig for catastrophic early disasters; but to content himself with the apparently insignificant, negligible to all but the patient: physical inroads undermining his patient's personal vanity. For nobody minds confessing to a desire to assassinate or rape: same thing in Psychoanalytical terminology; his nearest and dearest. They mostly take pride, on the contrary, in so violently stimulating a confession. But to confess to what secretly bothers him most: such as an unsightly growth of hair: or moult of hair; in the wrong domain of his shamed anatomy; or a raw abrasion in his private parts; or a sinister itching lump pushing up and out of his immentionable Infernos below; is too humiliating. Is beneath his precious dignity. Is nonetheless: because of its very ignoble, ignominious puniness; at the petty crux of his troubles.

So concentrate, dear Lay Brothers, on the sore boil: and ignore the octopus ulcer. For the root at back of the trouble has been traced to even so harmless a white lie as giving the wrong; naturally later; date of birth. Which only recently caused a beautiful Nordic model: when forced to betray her real age by long-nosed Killer Police; to lose her job. Then, as a direct consequence: to kill herself.

And further back, even more unbelievably, a *Nun*, of all people, did that very same thing. Having given an erroneous date of birth originally: two years out in the vain direction; she was so gnawed by conscience at her heinous sin of vanity, that she could bear the threat of flames no longer. So, in hopeless despair, she flung herself into the flames.

When the patient puts on a hysterical show of extended lament: like a plover decoying the hunter from its hidden nest of eggs; the Psycho Pedlar should bear firmly in mind that hysteria, like everything else, comes with practice. And his patient is merely running up and down the scales of his virtuosity.

There is no doubt that the Psycho Pedlars have done a great deal of reconstructive work. Especially in the cases of soldiers shell-shocked into idiocy. In spite of a few minor constructions collapsing entirely on the experimental road.

All progress after all; all breaking of fresh ground: breaking is undoubtedly the operative word here; is functionally bound to have its failures. Its thrown-out litter of lesser guinea pig carcases: on the upward stretch to achievement. From which to learn better next time.

But: since my personal experience in this progressive field has been far from extensive, I think that I must class myself as merely one of the unfortunate guinea pigs.

In the first place I went to a Roman P.P., whose perfect parody of an immaculately elegant, impeccably groomed gentleman: intimidated me to so frozen an extent, that I could not open my mouth: for sex, nor wasting away cash.

After five silent sittings, at five thousand lira the half-hour; face to bland face in a state of perfect detachment; both playing at: silence in the pig market, let the old sow speak first; I wrote him a polite letter to say I didn't think we were getting very far.

To which he replied, just as politely, that my difficulty, he had deduced: was inability to communicate.

So no more comment was made on the fruitless matter. In any case he had nothing to complain about; and no doubt wished all his guinea pigs were as speechless and passive.

In the second place, at some, bag of nerve, time later: for I had not exactly been encouraged at the first encounter; I went to an English P.P., who was encouragingly shabby and ugly: notwithstanding that he practised in Harley Street. It was more a case, on this promising occasion, of not being able to keep my mouth shut.

As soon as I pushed open the padded door, which swung to soundlessly after me; sat, in a distraught bundle of hair, dangling scarves, and winter paraphernalia, in the unavoidable writhing chair facing him; and saw his soberly understanding mug, cocked on one side, like a robin's expecting crumbs; I felt an enormous great apple core craning up my throat: and burst into a splurge of ungainly, spluttering down tears.

In the meantime, he leaned back indolently in his chair, stretched luxuriously, let out a stifled yawn, and fiddled with his watch chain. For indeed, for one who had witnessed as he had, so many times before, so many similar scenes of slowly wearing down resistance: it must have been intolerably tedious.

Then, tearing his benignly indifferent gaze at last, from the window on to his performing seal, he softly said: 'It is all right, you are doing very nicely; it is all in the pattern.'

But, by the time I had recovered from my inexplicable spasms: and composed myself enough to speak: wringing out five or six sodden handkerchiefs in the process; half my precious: six guinea an hour; time was gone.

Because every self-respecting guinea pig knows better than to arrive on the dot of its appointment; knows it must be at least a quarter of an hour late: if only for the sake of its identification. Or else how can the P.P. tell there is anything wrong with it.

It may also go so far as to miss an appointment altogether every now and then; but it is only a really classy guinea pig can afford the prestige of paying for a bodiless hour of torture. But, if it abuses of its privilege: by missing too often; the P.P. gets narky. It is not enough to be crazy, it must, to complete the picture: act crazy.

But I was determined, all the same, not to be so profitlessly dumb as at my previous interviews: if I had to crash down my stubborn battlements with a verbal pickaxe. So I searched arduously in my mind: void of present, past, or future; for a tempting morsel of the root extraordinary, to set before my king. For there is nothing kings like less, or despise more: than the inexcusable ordinary.

My past life stretched backwards in flat barren plains of criminal ordinaryness: without a single ridge of interesting abnormality to break up the grey symmetrical horizon.

My cold reserved family relations, long since cut off, summoned up no remotely dramatic incident. Nothing adequately sensational; sufficiently incestuous: to be worth laying bare, in its sensual gravy, on the table.

I was reduced: as I have no doubt many have been reduced before, when put to this gruelling test; to invention. To inventing the missing parts, and titivating up the inadequacies.

After getting myself into an inextricable tangle of inarticulacies; vainly trying to piece together dimly sighted, almost faded episodes; embellished and pepped up by either the deceptions of memory, or the hallucinations of dreams: a colourful smoke screen in which to envelop the crucial fingernail that I was intent on not being seen; my mentor solemnly announced: 'It is obvious, is it not: that you wish to kill your mother.'

To which unfounded accusation, I hotly expostulated that he was wrong; and hotly insisted, on the contrary, that it was my father I wished to kill. Undeterred by the minor detail: that he had already rubbed himself out: this long time ago.

But: he answered with a kindly smile: 'That cannot be, for it is not in the pattern. It is your father you wish to go to bed with; but your subconscious guilt has reversed the wish.'

It did not take me long either to learn: that if I said a 'specimen' that came up: in the course of our infantile dialogue: was white: it subconsciously meant that it was black. So I tried reversing my statements, and got back to where I started.

He would suddenly pounce on my most inconsequential 'specimens': that I had put in deliberately just to keep the desultory conversation from petering out; with the replete: Ah; of a boa constrictor that had swallowed an extra large goat: now *what* made you say that? Then he would proceed to explain what did, and fit it, as pleased as Punch, into his jigsaw puzzle. The filling of which was his special pet hobby.

So, at the end of the distinctly sticky sitting: as he was trying out a final recourse to mild hypnosis, in order to further weaken my resistance, with the leading soporific words: now just imagine yourself stretched out in a deck chair, relaxing in the wonderful sun-of-the-south . . . I decided to hand out to him a fitting, juicily enigmatic, 'specimen' for his delectation.

As I was making mock then, to be bemusedly coming to: for I had not, in truth, been 'out' for a split second, but could not offend his good will; I blurted out, as it were still under the influence: 'But I hate the sun! Can't you see that I hate the sun! I hate it! I hate it! That is the whole point. I mean the S.U.N. Not my own son of course.'

So saying, I left him ruminatively chewing on the play of words . . . For he saw at once that: sun; was but a transparent camouflage for: son.

When I got home: or to the rented barracks room in the Siberian wilds of Kilburn that I had no alternative but to call home; I was in a strangely discomposed, harassed and upset state; brought on by the demoralizing glut of delving, in spite of my reluctance to; into things better left undelved into. I was not going to be caught napping again, on the defensive, with no red herrings prepared to trail, to waylay, and put the hunter off the scent. So I spent the intervening nights intent on repairing the deficiencies, and discrepancies of my primary, pathetically insufficient, recital.

Knowing that it was his favourite dish: I concentrated exclusively on dirt. On all the disgusting things I could think of. Straining to its limits: my impoverished dirt box.

With praiseworthy labour, I fabricated, out of the fluff of hoovered-up stuffing in my head, obscene images. I endeavoured, with all the might of my mind, to embody the cancerous abysm of obscenity.

I did my eager best to transform the dried up husks of dead passions: into monstrous flowers of vitriolic succulence. The scattered empty peapods of my past: into still sappily-ripe erotic fruit.

I slept with a pad under my pillow to record, before it

escaped into limbo land, the unbroken thread of my dreams . . .

The queer thing was: that whereas before I could never remember beyond the waking readjustment, nor capture in print the magnified absurdities of my dreams: now they chugged out, all too humdrumly.

So I must be getting somewhere: although it looked more like the landscape of nowhere.

But, to my consternation, my miniature train: instead of taking me into a shocking mixed embroilment of crude sex, with all the corks of prudery drawn; went winding down all the small byways: the trifling tributary lines of diminishing domestic duties.

I was beset in my dreams with a recurring, maddening mania for tidying up, putting in place endless stacks of rubbish and junk: which had no appointed place to be put in. Repeatedly trying to make order in a permanent squalor dump in which order refused to be made. The continual abortive effort of a sexless mouse.

It was most disappointing; and more boring than life itself. For, while faithfully preserving all its representational exactitude, it never came to an end: till I woke up in a sweat of petulant pedantry. And: though highly significant no doubt; this shaming material would never do.

I could never produce, for his spitting out contempt, such a paucity of liplicking plums: such an insignificant mouthful of dust. It would undoubtedly have to be suppressed without delay; and substituted by something more flavoursome.

So; notwithstanding my temporary setbacks, I collected, and conscientiously wrote down: quite an impressive document of pulped slime. With an ambiguous emphasis on Lesbianism; and an ambivalent leaning towards bestiality. I was hoping the latter was a new vice for him; as he had not confronted me with it up till now: on his list of probables.

Thereupon, at the next sitting, praying for my courage not to fail me: with the cunning ingenuity of a fox in a corner; I pulled out my scribbled papers and said casually: 'I made a few notes to help you.'

Then I started, stumblingly, to read: because I never could have said spontaneously such self committing things. Spontaneity being no pal of minc.

I have got to compliment myself that the results of my reading: more than justified my nightly efforts. To say the least: they were beamingly gratifying. For, if ever a P.P. can be said to beam: mine beamed, widely. If not quite from ear to ear.

He turned all at once, from a hostile stranger, into a long lost buddy. Almost banged me on the back in his enthusiasm, and heartily congratulated me: saying I deserved a medal. Presumably a Dirt one. 'Two or three more gallops of release in the open like that one:' he went on; 'and you will be over the worst hurdles of repression. You are very nearly in the clear now, and well on the way to victory.

'What did I say: by coming forward so liberally, and doing it all yourself, you have proved that you are your own best doctor.'

'But;' I remonstrated meekly; 'in that case why do I bother to go to you?'

I was arrested by the boa constrictor's: Ah; again. Extra prolonged to conceal his dilemma . . . But there were no bed bugs on him: he knew his cue bang off. So, with deprecating modesty, he now replied: 'My part is but to wait and watch, to see what happens. Yours is to make it happen. You must do all the work yourself; I can but show you the way, and explain the pattern to you afterwards.'

Which accursed pattern: after my last exhaustive bout; he proceeded to complacently explain. He had me tied up, in a jiffy, into a neat, cellophane wrapped, parcel; clearly labelled, in block letters: *Bestial Lesbian.*

To get closer to the radical twist in my perversion: he questioned me closely concerning my first seduction by a woman. But, rack my brains as I did: on the spur of the moment, I could not conjure up an appropriate scene. Although he had me fully convinced, by the end: that there was such a seduction scene; tucked away in my subconscious. Lurking in fright from my conscious condemnation. Which no doubt would reveal itself in its own, analysed out of concealment, time.

As for the 'Bestial' part of the label on the parcel: I do honestly believe it gave him a bit of a turn. For he brushed it aside a trifle hurriedly. Although, of course, he was much too broadminded to show it obviously. And, to reassure me: with his complete lack of conventional prejudice; he confided conspiratorially: 'I too, used to sleep with a kitten on my stomach as a child; and it was a very pleasant sensation I remember. We all do these things, it is nothing to worry about.'

Finally: increasingly irritated by my continuous wriggling and fidgeting, in embarrassment: under his man to man scrutiny; he turned on me, in admonishing reproval. 'Until you can look me in the eyes, and treat me like a Man, instead of a mistrustful enemy:' he announced; 'you will not be able to gain maturity, nor get over your crushing inferiority complex.'

He was perfectly right in saying that I never did deliberately look at him, anything but. Although, without looking, I seemed to see enough of him. But surely it was hardly a 'Man' I was after; and, had I been, the P.P.'s lair was hardly the place to look for one.

What I wanted was the opposite of a Man: from whose

interventions all my troubles had sprung. I wanted a supremely superior, spiritually inspired, castrated male eunuch.

But perhaps my maladjustment, and embarrassment in the presence of my P.P., was due to the famous 'transference' exchange, not having got to work yet. And I have to regretfully announce, to my fault and my loss, that it never did.

Nor can I accuse my P.P. of ever being guilty of the famous amorous pouncings: I had heard so graphically about; at the rounding up of a particularly pitiful interview. If mine had pounced at all, it would most certainly have been with a brandished hatchet in his hand.

At our parting interview indeed: because it was impossible to keep the argument going when I had scraped to the bottom of my vat of abscesses; he asked me with secret intent: 'Have you ever thought seriously about death, Mrs. Thomas?' To which I answered as seriously: looking him straight in the eye for the first time: 'I think of nothing else with you, Mr. Ambivalence.'

I felt I had not failed him at last; and got the last word in as well.

The final interview was closed. There was nothing more, for either of us to say. It remained but for him to send in the bill. And but for me not to pay it.

But anyhow my broken fingernail was still safely hidden away: still broken intact. And my P.P. prober had never discovered the break. My precious immature discontent could still stroll abroad, in nagging familiarity: unmolested by the peace healers.

It is a well known oddity that people both want to be cured, and don't want to be cured. They are afraid that, by removing their baby of wrongs, they will be left empty handed, with nothing left to nurse.

The Professional Man

Like most susceptible little women; I have a surrendering weakness for Professional Men. Most childishly weak for Doctors. Who, in spite of the popular scepticism, for their witch-doctor powers, that they enjoy today; and in spite of my own cynical disbelief in retrospect: when out of their intoning spell; still succeed in conveying by their clean-shaven, faintly lavender powdered faces, cologne pomaded, greying at the temples hair; brisk and efficient, while jokingly rallying manner: turning one's mountain into a molehill; by their expensive, retiringly checked exteriors; and by their impressively pompous bearing: black bag and stethoscope, carried as offhandedly as a superfluous vanity case and parasol; a feeling of temporary reassurance.

Thus, every susceptible little woman feels: that one so trained in the body's displeasures; must consequently professionally understand: what are the body's exact technical pleasures.

The only antidote arising in her happy speculations, being as to whether: since he is so repulsively intimate with the lower disfunctionings of the body; can he possibly, yet be capable of feeling romantically inclined towards his lugubrious workshop.

Will his technical knowledge ruin or enhance his technique as a lover.

She has been informed: on other susceptible little women's authority; that he does not connect his workshop with a woman detached from his job, when he is courting.

But, although in her weak subjection to him, she longs for him to experiment; he, on the contrary, seems singularly uninterested. As though she were merely a faulty machine: he is tinkering with in his workshop. Which, of course, adds enormously: to his unapproachable sphinx fascination.

So I am afraid I can't clear up this dilemma for you. Although I think it must be a nice change to have somebody who knows what they are doing: if not passionately doing it. Rather than a passionate bungler.

The Dentist

It is stating the obvious to say that the Doctor's understudy; his stooge the Dentist; has no hope: in howling toothed, creation; of coming into the Doctor's romantic category.

For, however devastatingly dazzling he may be; no little woman is prepared to sacrifice her vanity, to the extent of attempting a winning flirtation: with her jaw prised open, her face sweating with contraction, her eyes screwed up, her voice squawking raucously with piercing drilling pain, and an accumulation of saliva gurgling and gasping into a rubber sucking tube: stuck carelessly, catching on to her dry swollen tongue; into the tender crevices of her unheeded, cotton-wool-stuffed, bleeding gums. For her chances are not sanguine: with such a sanguinary sadist bending over her, and sadistically attending to her excavations and extractions.

The unanswerable conundrum is: whatever could have made a Dentist choose to be a Dentist.

Or a Pedicurist a Pedicurist: as far as that goes. There is no limit to the objectionable environments; and repulsive parts and innards of the body: that men voluntarily choose: to dedicate their daylight dreams to.

It can only be: the nostalgia of the offal; that accounts for it

The Police

Or, even more bafflingly: whatever can have made a sane man choose to be a Policeman. Unless it is that his level of intelligence is so moronically low: that it makes no other choice conceivable.

But then again I am made to credit: that quite a number of these presumptuously strutting, buttoned-up nobodys; misguidedly believe that it is a noble profession. As inspired with missionary zeal as the Priesthood.

They devoutly shine and glisten with bristling keenness for promotion: at the cost of victimizing innocent citizens over pedantically insignificant breaches of the Law; as though it were a celestial ascension.

The major part however of this gangster race are nothing more celestial: than gangsters in reverse. Who: but for the false pride of their authoritative uniforms; would be securely locked up themselves; in their prison homes from home. Where they rightfully belong: if anybody does.

So, like all reformed vice practisers, they zealously treat the unreformed with a spate of uncontrollable, punishing viciousness. To make up for their own disciplined abstention: from punishable vice.

Notwithstanding that it is possible to meet, on diverse occasions: a pleasant obliging policeman, unvitiated by avenging rancour: you personally must observe, as a matter of strict principle, a steadfast moral loathing of their ignorant power: used as a legal weapon; to do as they wilfully will. Of their bullying methods: to jog up their own failing courage; against the solitary powerlessness of the individual. However eminent an individual he is: in his own solitary eminence.

So, just as you must love the persecuted peoples on principle: regardless of personal antipathy; so you must loathe these rosy favoured: by no reason of their own merit; downers of personal independence in the name of the Law. Who grow fat on the culpability of the deprived rebellious.

When it comes to the gruesome depths of policewomen: for sheer hideous venom; for no self-respecting woman not so grotesquely unfortunate by birth; or kangaroo shapeless by nature: would contemplate caricaturing herself even more grotesquely; they surpass: by a long rope corded neck; the worst male tyrants.

The Lawyers

Before concluding my list of types of people that you might conceivably encounter at the party: or on your journeyings elsewhere; I must make a final obituary: a last little epitaph; to the diplomatic evasions of Solicitors.

Diplomatic evasions which could more pertinently be called: skilled and gifted lying. For of all lying experts: not excluding the Sicilian or Welsh; the foxwily Solicitor is, without pinch of doubt; the most phenomenal exponent of lying.

Because he is taught by profession to lie. Therefore the lie is grafted: as a sapling is grafted into the maturer bark of a treetrunk; into a formalized style: an accepted formula. An intricate system of trained fact-twisting: twisting them into looking the opposite of what they originally were. With in addition: as a verbal ornamentation to his disarming plea; a natural, dishonest to God, gift of the gab. To make his sly sidestepping of the awkward point: go down more smoothly sugar-coated.

So, kindly note, he is not a man to be ignored; and can be: as long as you keep on the right side of him in tricky situations; a valuable connection. As long as his legal deceit is on your side: not directed to proving you wrong.

But I have never grasped: if both sides in a law case are legally permitted to lie, like brilliantly literate troupers; how any appropriate verdict is ever reached in the end. When a verdict eventually is reached however: it has no crude connection with truth or justice. It appears to be a question of: who can afford to pay the most formidable liar in the racket.

He is a perilous man too, in that: as a leading part in his wage-winning role; he must have a certain canny way with him: a falsely enchanting slippery charm. If only of temporary, speaking duration.

Unfortunately when off duty; he is still defensively on duty. He is fearful of dropping his cultivated suave unruffled pretence. So deeply ingrained has it become in his no longer real personality.

So that he is virtually incapacitated from ever behaving naturally and freely. Let alone doing anything so controversial as telling the naked untellable truth.

He is wound up in his skein of multi-coloured tangled wool: as inextricably as a precociously fencing kitten.

For all his boldness of sweeping rhetoric in the Courtroom; his hair-splitting invective; his indignant fervour of abuse: against the heinous crimes of his opponent; he is, in private, a fearful, hiding man. Crouching in his burrow: practising his legal lines for his next public appearance.

He squeamishly hates: the dirty revealing facts of life; because his living is made evading and misrepresenting them.

Because he lives flamboyantly in public scenes: he cannot bear, even the kindling crackling of a private scene.

Mocking-bird jolly on his derisive exterior. With a malignant canker of worm-burrowing preoccupations: eating him up underneath.

As for a heart: if he ever had one; it is concealed and congealed out of all existence.

Never hope for, then: a romance with a Solicitor. For he will only switch on his insuperable combination of maddening evasion and delaying tactics. Since he has no intention, in his immunity: of being taken in. And you will find yourself at the epilogue; precisely where you were at the prologue: out in the foggy foggy dew.

He would prefer to be committed to celibacy for a life sentence: rather than give a straight, committing himself, answer. The one absolute 'not done' Holy law: for a solicitor.

He is the original model of denial for a bachelor. With all the professional arts thrown in gratis: for denying the importunities of women.

Invulnerable undoubtedly; but how much is his invulnerability worth: the price of inhumanity.

VII

The Butcher: The Baker; The Candlestick Maker

What with the matrimonial disadvantages of the previous, more sophisticated types; it might be more provident: for you to angle for a straightforward, exceptionally generous, tradesman. Provided, that is, he has enough put by: in a slavering heap in the bank; for the extravagant desires of both of us.

And forget all about the vampish lures into High Society. Which, even if it exists any more, is hopelessly out of date; financially diminished; and, I have no doubt, excessively deadly.

For the vaunted ideal life of lengthy leisure; pottering and dabbling idleness; is, I think we agree, both demoralizing to the spirit and softening to the body.

There is no savour left in too much of a good thing. The good thing has got to be penitentially worked for: to obtain its real, rewarding relish. Then, even the littlest treats, taste like feasts.

Tradesmen too have each their own separate savour: created by sustained allegiance to their hereditary trades.

The Baker suggests in his person the floury nocturnal whiteness of his sweated, kneading labours, in the glowing stoking ovens of our sleeping night. He recalls the childhood nostalgic longing odour: of hot crusty softly crumbling, sweetly mouth-watering, new-baked bread; in the famished morning.

He conjures up all the motherly warmth of smothering breast comfort; that a child misses so yearningly in after life.

It is perfectly irrelevant to this benign impression he makes; that the Baker in reality, is nearly always a most unhealthy man. A wretched, malformed, hollowed-in consumptive: from working under such murderous conditions to his endurance and stamina.

That he is driven: in his purgatorial furnaces; to take constant, consecutive swigs of liquid. For his thirst is unquenchable; and the nightly strain he undergoes, makes the liquid necessarily alcoholic.

So the omnipotent provider of the entire world is: as omnipotent providers are apt to be; a sorry hunchbacked contradiction of the golden crackling riches that he provides.

It has always been one of my many unfulfilled ambitions to live in a room bang over a bakehouse. To lie all the winter stewing in that delicious rising heat; and dreaming in that dreamy, wafted up fragrance of bread.

I feel that life could offer no more, in sensual delights; and I should never want to move again out of my levitation between the fires of the earth: and the resurrecting fumes of Heaven.

But, like a lot of the simplest things one passionately wants, it is impossible to attain.

These dim, obscure, mysterious interiors: counterparts of the Baker's interior; where tradesmen work; and which they construct into a working home background: so much more sympathetic than any planned parlour for visitor's adulation; always fill me with covetous wonder. And I always wish that I too could obtain such a telling background: without being put through the old treadmill of learning their arduous trade. (The old story of the Bisto kids and the gravy, I'm afraid.)

What is there more visually paintable; more symmetrically satisfactory; more atmospherically stimulating, in co-ordinated movement; more welcoming to the thirsting soul: than *The Blacksmith's Forge*. With its black recesses; its red sparking fires; its reanimating, giant puffing bellows.

With its friendly or frisky horses having their new iron shoes soldered into their planed-down hooves; accompanied by a burning acrid stench. Or: haltered to posts in downtrodden shabbiness, passively waiting their turn. Or: already shod and upstage; their hooves gleaming with smartly-turned-out, going-to-town varnish.

It is a social meeting place where local big heads meet: out of the shivering wind and shuddering rain; to discuss the scandalous news. And to exchange unreal, impotently indignant politics. Shouting above the clatter and hammering: of scarlet melting lengths of beaten-to-death iron. Slashed and coaxed into horseshoe roundness; and punched into holes. In readiness for long nails deftly inserted into the unfeeling, giving-in deadness of the hoof.

While the birdnesting swallows and swifts dart domestically in and out of the cobwebby beams. Encrusted with hanging upside down bats: dozing in anticipation of the night's verminous adventures.

The soot and iron dusted Blacksmith: with his lesser, toned down and toning in, shirtsleeved apprentices: clock working impersonally. Like some long ago classical figures in a children's story book.

What is more evocatively suggestive to the country bedded mind than: *The Cobbler's* leathery smelling den. With a miscellanouse conglomeration of every meticulous or careless description of shoes. A tattily discarded, or bravely renovated brothel: of hopeless 'has been' footwear. With: on top of the pile of has beens; a pair of immaculately soled, and purification uppered feet: aspiringly making a fresh start.

More picturesquely Bible reminiscent than *The Carpenter's* shed of Joseph's and Christ's; doing all that Joseph and Christ were supposed to do. Manually handling the virtue of God's wood; so that its quality and strength of character passes into them: as Prophets in the wood. Prophetically reading the grained circles of ageing time: in the hacked open clock face of the wooden suffering treetrunk.

And above all: what is more homely welcoming than the promising intimacy of the Pub. With its replenishing cellars icily inviting more: in warming promise below.

Having spent a bad half of my life literally inside pubs; where at the beginning I suffered a choking claustrophobia, trapped from the running freedom of out-of-doors. Longing: from the bottom of my hobnailed hopping boots; to ride my stinking stagnation: down the wild winds of steeply diving, riding hills. To roll my bloated with booze body, clogged with stultifying talk: in purple haze heather, yellow gorse prickly, beech and birch wooded: bramble and broom copsed moors. Screeching with the supernatural cries of exotic feathered pheasants; finery winged jays; hooded owls hooting in the barky darkness of hiding crevices. Grieving with the lamenting cries of stealing magpies; with their thieves' hoard of ring glitter in a stick woven basket nest. Perched aloft alone: in the highest inaccessible tree; with the fewest climbing up branches. Out of pilfering reach of envious neighbours.

And all the multitudinous, shrilly echoing; creeping and pecking bird noises. Slinking in the undergrowth, crawling and twig-cracking animal noises. Insect infested, ticking, hissing and clicking. Droning and buzzing noises of the lovely lost, leaf fluttering province. The breathing province: of my breeze pulsing country being. Now lost for me irretrievably: in the murky enclosure of pubs.

I ravenously craved: like a hunting hound shut in a tent in the desert; for sharp green blades of grass. Reed squelching rushy bogs; pebble jingling, and hurriedly rattling on streams. With brown spotted trouts cowering under the shadowy banks, to breathtakingly tickle, under their bellies, to stillness. And flashy blue kingfishers, flashing over from catkined willows; plenteously replete with fishy regurgitations for their squawking, gaping-beaked fledglings. To their armlong nesting holes lined with reeking fishbones; under the protecting roots of the overhanging oak.

Then cuckoos of course; repetitiously cuckooing away; like inferior Beethovens.

But gradually I got used to pubbing: as easily as to most pernicious habits. Gradually the noisy, tapped and lamped cosiness; the smoky soup enveloping, gravy thick fug of the pub: enveloped me too, within its seducing spell. Its shining rows of villainous bottles; its wicked clinking glasses of manufactured friendship; its muzzy bumbling customers under an unaccustomed escaping aspect: began to gradually seduce me. But more still: the burning upward rush to the head; then the lullabying coma of the alcohol: held me a fast prisoner.

Without my idiotic rout of senses ever dreaming of bothering to pause; and consider the ultimate damage that it must inevitably do to us.

Without it ever entering my barrel blind; my donkey blinkered head; to moderate our consumption. Let alone to stop altogether. Nor even to try to make an abortive effort to reform us; and save the lining of our skins in time.

Till, in the end, the pub became for me: and more so even for Dylan; a home: more homely than our own;

from home. I can't remember one isolated evening that we spent at home: for the simple reason that I don't think there ever was one.

To contemplate living without a pub to go back to; was homelessness indeed. A long, homeless blank to fill up; like a sheet of blank paper with no inspiration. With no boozing pals in it, to fill it with homely life.

Therefore, perhaps the greatest sacrifice that I have ever made: or, to be accurate, undoubtedly the greatest; has been, with the utmost difficulty: keeping out of pubs.

But, as they say, you never know what you can do till you try.

That is true, up to a point; but, while stopping the action of going home; it does not stop the homing instinct.

Which shows itself in all sorts of queer aberrations; second best antidotes; compensatory consolations. Such as: bar fly sticking to chromium-new; spit and polished; shinily dismissing foreign bars. Sipping invisible measures of sickly liqueurs: under fierce Latin disapproval. Which: if one has the temerity to push forward the glass for more; looks in horrified disbelief at you, and shrieks: what, ANOTHER? With nothing; not one homely grubby corner; of a pub in them. While trying to pretend in vain; that it has the remote nostalgic sensation of an old and ugly pub.

Not from choice; but, as the desperately high price of survival. The only means of obtaining this eyeteeth extraction of myself from publand; has been to leave the land of homing pubs.

To the truly addicted pubgoers: they have an indefinable something of the same liberation as in a home. But better: because it is a home that is blessedly not one's own. Nor anybody's home: but the Landlord's. So that it belongs freely, with no obligations, to everybody: who can pay for it.

An indefinable warmth of attraction: which is dismally lacking in the bleak entertainments of private houses: from which one cannot escape at surfeited will. Thrifty prisons of genteelly chatting mock sociability; which we always avoided on principle. While being mutually avoided ourselves: by nervous, upper-class hosts. Who, with legitimate reason, never knew what we might do next; in the breakages of launched-through-the-air, frail porcelain.

So that; by giving up pubs; I was, at the same time, giving up all my previous old acquaintances. And cutting myself off in a peopleless world: as far as I was concerned. With no people I knew in it; and not a whiff, or a sniff of a scent, of social life: high or low.

No foreigner is capable of seeing, or understanding: the strong pull that pubs have, for the British, to get together. Mostly away from the family; in the rejoicing irresponsibility of insobriety. Or can credit their eyes at the sudden unexpected change; from the Britisher's typical dour bearing, and sour replies; to his free and easy, voluble conviviality. For there is no visible relationship between the two.

The Foreigner: who has been uniformly socially accessible all along: if anything, even brighter in the early morning before a drink; merely wants to get out, as fast as possible: from such a depressing, messy dump; ruining his precious health, and wasting his precious time.

So this is really a final admonition to you: to try to be like the foreigner, in his disparaging attitude towards pubs. Who knows that it is best for his love life; for his love of eating and sleeping life; but, most worshipfully: for his wallet's life; not to go into pubs.

Otherwise you, who are British: but have also weathered the barren abstemiousnesses of living abroad; might fatally develop too, the same pub sickness. As perilously streaming into the veins as a snake bite: and as perilous to staunch.

A pub sickness, that is more than a homesickness: that is a sickness unto returning into death. For pubs are the spiritual homes of a death of the spirit. They reanimate the already dead with the same spirit that assassinated them. Only to assassinate them anew.

But to return to the individual aromas of differing trades; it would be more prudent for you: who are so keen on fresh air, and always open windows blasting everybody out of the house; and who are so squeamish at the sight of slaughtered carcases; to keep well away from the terror-fraught realism: it seems but a minute since the still warmly throbbing, freshly skinned animals were shocked to death; of the *Butcher's* raw meatiness.

The anxious animals; huddled together in closed suspicion; instinctively sense, by smell, too late, the contagion of panic fear: at the piercing reek of consecutive quick knifings. Imposing: even when it is all over, and they are laid out helpless on the Butcher's carving up slab; a pervading stink of guilty massacre. Worrying the nostrils, twitching with distaste, of the greedy meat consumer.

So we may safely rub out the Butcher: as meatily not your meat.

From similar motives of squeamishness: but for different fish aromatic provocations; it would be prudent for you as well: to prudently keep away from the *Fishmonger's* dripping with filthy slime hands, and smeared with fish scales apron. Although his fishes have none of the meat's overpowering resemblance to a human mortuary.

For, knowing your susceptibilities, you have only got to see him once: gaily slashing off the eye-goggling fish heads; frivolously snicking off the limp fish-tails; snipping and trimming off the fins, like a born with the scissors seamstress; then, with a lightning nick, and dexterous slit up the fish's bowels; scooping out a slithering pile of bloody, worming round, live maggot guts: for you to pass straight out; and faint in a basin of serpentine eels. Conveniently slipping to catch you, on the slippery fished floor.

So we may also perfunctorily dismiss the fishy embraces of so slippery a lovemonger.

As for the *Candlestick Maker*; lovable as he sounds; I am afraid that, for lack of candles nowadays in the home: only flickering faithfully still at the Altar; and consequently the demand for candlesticks: except perhaps in a few last remaining cabins in the remotest Western bogs; the poor Devil is extinct.

As extinct as the Patcher Up of venereal diseases: for lack of faulty candles to patch up any more. So they are both now penuriously out of business.

No, I think a nice, clean, brisk, well-to-do *Grocer*: with a profitably bowler-hatted paunch; and a plentiful supply of substantial stores to fall back on: as though for a starving siege in the never knowing, unpredictable future: would be a lot more suitable for us.

Devoted to us, of course; and gifted at miscounting the change in our favour. While simultaneously handing out to us a generous share of the profits. As proper: anybody can see we are real; Ladies deserve.

A cut above himself, that we can maliciously use to cut him down, to humble him: whenever he tends to get above himself.

To keep him forever: in striving upward awe of our superior, if penniless standing as real Ladies. To never let him forget: by constant deflating pricks, of his gaining composure, in down to earth browsing familiarity; that we are accustomed to 'better things'. No need to go into details of what the 'better things' were. So he must keep up our appearances: in order to show that he is good enough for us.

To better his own position: as an up and coming Gentleman: he must, in honour bound, provide for us: the 'better things'. It is always better to be the legend labelled 'better': than the unlabelled secondary reflector of the legend. Even if, in reality, the reflector is unquestionably the 'better' of the two.

Having got our Grocer nicely tied up in this fat legend of labels; he won't get out easily from under. But we must beware that Grocers are as crafty as rats in a trap: when it comes to gnawing their way out of a sack of corn.

The discouraging snag in our act: is that it is too easy to be a Perfect Lady. Awfully miserable, and apathetically paralysing too. It is purely and simply: or, to be more exact, hardly and grimly; an act of keeping one's mouth hermetically sealed in public: to all but agreeable hypocrisies. While nagging the pants off in private.

For how many hermetically sealed months in woman-downing, but to set them up, Italy; have I been referred to benignly as: '*questa gentilissima Signora; si vede é una persona per bene; con la faccia d'angelo: tanto fine . . .*'

Or simpering words to that sloppily untrue effect: as though bestowing upon me a sacred cow untouchability.

Only to diffidently open my mouth once; and stumblingly start to speak what I think; to be contemptuously shrugged off as: that pitiful thing that knows not what she says. '*Che peccato: fa pietà.*' Making so little of herself . . . Then they commiseratingly advise me to go into a nice Clinic for deranged Gentlewomen: '*per un lungo riposo: per calmarsi i nervi.*'

Which I feel will be a very long rest indeed; but doubt if my nerves will be calmed.

'Ah, but they are not really to blame, perhaps,' they

go on, with a nauseous let up of relenting charity: 'it is the fault of their men. Who are all: without exception; impotent drunkards, or pederasts, in Anglo-Saxon madhouses. So what can you expect: they need a real man to look after them.'

It does not require much stretch of imagination to guess who are the 'real men'.

The crucial difference in this exhibiting respect: between a Celtic Lady and a Latin Lady: is that the former one exhibits in public. Gives her Fiends of Hell: their heads in the open air; exercises them out of doors; enjoys putting them at the jumps of argument. An argument to her is not an offence; as with the Latins; but a stimulation.

Whereas the latter one keeps her Fiends of Hell firmly suppressed, under a close guard, in public. But organizes them: all the more fiendishly, for her private ends; in privacy. For the tyrannies of tenacious intimacy.

There is no measurable difference in the tongue sting of the Fiends. Although I am inclined to think, naturally enough: that private tyranny is worse than public tyranny.

Or, if we fail to hold on to our commendable Grocer: with our Ladylike wiles and guile; would it be too lowering to our dignity, do you think, to descend to the stuffy level of a dandy, cravenly ambitious *Draper*. As astute as a whistling kettle of Welshmen: whistling, even the Jews, out of competition.

But I fear that we could never stand his smarming servility; his arse-licking civility; his tasty refainments of skin-fitting dress. His pansy airs and graces; his pursed lips of genteelly pinched vowels: melodiously wooing the tough customers for their reluctant capitulation.

We would have but to visualize him: after the shopping day's babblings and flutings; in prospective ordeal. In his elastic-banded shirtsleeves and fancy tie; round shouldered from excessive bowing and scraping; bent double over his account books. Totting up, with demon whispering accuracy, his nightly eleven-three-farthings of profit. To be sufficiently deterred at the start: by the indecent vision.

Then later: but to visualize him more indecently still: after a frugal supper of dieting greens, to purge his constipated line of bulging contours; on his way to bed. Having now also modestly removed: besides his best selling jacket; and fixed in their knife-edged creases, his shiny pin-striped trousers. Prowling and pricing: pleased as a chill-proofed pumpkin, in his lamb's wool cuddling combinations; round his suffocating Cloth Hall. Gloating on his glut of clothing: for the vulgar unclothed. To be chilled to our marrows.

But to be forced to observe: with ill-concealed revulsion; his indoor tapeworm body, obscenely wobbling under the cosseting wool. His flabby puffed chalk-white, tentacled hands: from so avidly grasping his gains. His spreading webbed feet, squeezed into too tighly creaking shoes; from so long static standing behind the counter. To be thoroughly put off: for unbearably coarse life.

But then I don't suppose either for an illusory moment, that he could tolerate us; and our rough and ready Country ways. Any more readily than we could tolerate him, and his smooth and unctuous Town ways.

It is impossible to mix the rough with the smooth into a blended batter; for the rough always shows through at the end. Uppermost in the uncongenial blending.

It is no good our trying to insinuate our broad, Country strong upbringing: into the crushing Town corset of narrow, side by side, hooked and eyed, crushed together over-hanging slots. Because we are overwhelmed by a feeling of blowing up constriction; followed by an imminent explosion of contaminated steam.

So we shall have to get somebody from the Country: as root bedded in the Country as ourselves. And all Dylan's farming ancestors way back in pastoral Wales.

As earthily belonging; as crudely uncouth; as fat and jovial: as the Proverbial Farmer is made out to be; but never is.

For the trouble is: between the wooden, whiskered gruff, shouting bluff farmer: with his paintbox farm, and his painted imaginary animals; and the living embodiment of the romantic Proverb: is an unbridgeable discrepancy. A gap as wide as that between clean imaginary Heaven: and dirty living Earth.

The living earthy *Farmer*, is but a stingy small money-scraping step removed: from a bestial farm labourer. And remains, at granite heart, the same whipped cur getting his own back. By whipping his recently acquired underlings, with the cringing underdog's resentful fury: of his own recent liberation. He retains the same beaten down resentful: stoned numbskull of grumbling persecutions: as his master before him.

Growling his accumulated wrongs: of the weather, of the crops, of the prices: of his ill-fated abused, unwinnable battle with the land. With the land that is his enemy: out to best him. But an enemy to whom he is undetachably wedded: as to a strenuous trial of a wife. Who makes an ordeal of wrongs of his hopeless life; with never a sun or rain of hope: in his permanent drought.

It is against all the superstitious rules of his fearful nature; for a Farmer ever to dare to be so bold, as to show a hope of good in his land. Which vain presumption would instantly cause: a storm of such violence; that all his lands and hopes would be wrathfully flooded.

When next time, therefore, you start again: to rave to me about the beauties and joys of living on a farm; please get into your sweetly unrealistic head, that your romantic envisagings: though authentic, in a ruthlessly modified, muddily besmirched form; bear no startling resemblance to the frozen quagmire of congealed manure: in the muck and piss-pooled stable yard. That will confront you in the frosty rigours of the still dusk hours, in marble-still wintertime.

Bear severely then in your wandering mind: those brutal rising hours before dawn. As though dawn was not bleak enough to begin the day. As cruel as the pointless, purely sadistic waking, and sitting bolt upright, of sick sleeping patients; at five o'clock in the morning, in penitentiary Hospitals. Rigidly to enforce the military order: of sitting them in the same penitential position: for the rest of the relentlessly prolonged day. A day with no beginning and no end. No getting up and no going to bed. No light and no darkness. For the static planted: timelessly statued patients. Whose world's circumference is spent within the desert island of the bed, isolated by hemming-in precipices of mass animosity.

By destroying the soul of the patient: they succeed in destroying also, in sympathy; the body.

Though I should hesitate, for a lengthy period, to call us civilized; nevertheless we are far too spoiled by our undisciplined upbringings; and over-pampered in our lazy habits: to be capable of withstanding the undeviating monotony on a farm. Demanding fabulous resistance and endurance.

We could never tackle regularly: with never any variation or respite; the unrelenting bleakness of the dismal dawning day. The first sleepy glimpses: through gummed-up-with-protest eyes; of the starkly abandoned, left to rot in the ground, old decaying teeth stalks of past harvests. Never stick the frosty feel of rigid, stiffly crunching stubble underfoot. The glassy puddles crackling with splintered ice: under our chilblained feet. Or put up with our raw hands cracking at the touch of cold metal buckets. Our blue flesh goose-pimpling in responsive sympathy. And our puffing breaths making chimney smoke in the rednosed morning.

There are such phenomena as Gentlemen Farmers: scattered educationally over the farming landscape. Who are tweedily; and in their burly barking geniality: bags more similar to the fabled genuine article. Displaying: in their unwearable-out Harris tweeds; striding Wellington boots; and deliberate carelessness of torn, conspicuously patched up working togs: with farm dirt picturesquely applied by hand; all the open handed, go-ahead enthusiasm attributed to their genial characteristics. That the authentic sour, crabbed and mean Farmer: in generations old, Clergyman black suit, as undetachable from him as a second skin; conspicuously lacks.

So the Gentleman improved Farmer; with a differentiating soaped cleanliness below: from the original unsoaped below or above model; might be the guffawing answer to our abortive search for the ideal husband.

Slightly marred however: or, to be critical, more than slightly marred; by his appallingly educated, Public School accent. For a galling voice; and an ecstatically giving up the ghost B.B.C. pronunciation; may seem to you small drawbacks to fret against. But, I assure you, when continually wailing and bleating into your shuddering shut ear drums: in the constant inescapable communion of marriage: they become far from small drawbacks. But, on the contrary: maddening menaces of frightful dimensions. Unfairly obliterating all the other generous impulses of the individual. And, you will be inclined to decide that the stuck pig farmer: monosyllabically grunting, at five grunts an hour; would have been delightfully preferable after all.

It is true the Gentleman farmer enjoys the refinements

of delicate foods and rare wines. He knows how to take his liquor: and how to hold it. And will always be plausibly presentable: and passably articulate; in company.

Whereas the old fashioned avaricious rooting type: burying his pot of coined pounds under the flagstones; is content to get along with such low-class dishes as: faggots and tinned peas; tripe and onions; boiled side of bacon, cabbage, and parsley sauce. Incidentally all most delicious: bar the tinned peas. Or simply a saucepan of spuds and butter; with a heaped plate of bread and butter at the side. All washed down with Old and Mild. Or, more often, with thick tea, stewed leather tan: with a good inch of sugar at the bottom of the cup.

The two commodities he primitively fears are: fresh vegetables: apart from the traditional cabbage; and fresh fruit. Although a nice tin of fruit is a treat for Sundays.

As for his gifts in company: his illiterate speech will be stuttering slow, and doggedly dogmatic. Centering undeviatingly on how much more profit can he wring out: of his already wrung-out threadbare plot of land.

So it is no good expecting him to suddenly burgeon into Oscar Wilde fluency and brilliance.

As a further inducement for the Gentleman; presumably his lovemaking performance in the marriage bed is appreciably more frequent in action. More sensitive in treatment; and more sophisticated in variations: than the mole-blind rooting in obscurity of the original farmer. For whom such sensual pleasures represent: a dirty orgy saved up for Saturday night. In view of the exceptional lying later in bed, repose: permitted once a week on Sunday mornings.

He will probably not distinguish your indistinguishably shaggy coated in the cold body: from one of his own, shaggy coated in the cold, ewes in his breeding pen.

For he has never seen a shorn naked woman; and would be deeply horrified at the unclean thought.

As far as nakedness goes; neither has he ever seen a shorn naked man. For the only tenacious leech of clothing: that he peels unwillingly off himself; is his glued together trousers. Apart from his Gorgonzola boots; which he also usually remembers to take off. For the sake of saving wear and tear: of the leather, and the sheets.

But otherwise he religiously sticks to his scratchy flannel shirt, reaching down to his knees: come heatwave, come earthquake.

But then Gentlemanly refinements in love: are not everything either. And the petty annoyances of laid on, with a sugar tongs, refinement: can justifiably outweigh the physical offence of crude violation. Which at least has the inestimable merit: of not being, in the least, personal.

But I cannot seriously advocate the original Farmer: in preference to the Gentleman Farmer. Because his lack of any finer sensation: let alone elementary sanitation; any ameliorating nicenesses; or any mental communion whatever would inevitably get you flagstone down in the end.

The primitive is very beautiful in fictitious theory; but very desolate in empty practice.

Our Gentleman Farmer however, should combine the best of both worlds: working in the country combined with emancipated relaxation. And: disregarding irritating mannerisms, picked up from a tyrannic archaic education, for which he is not to blame; would be as near perfection as we could hope to get. Especially if he could cook as well; but I suppose that is really asking too much. Not suitable anyhow for our rugged bearskin hugging Farmer.

We shall have to obtain that almost extinct treasure: a large comfortable body in heavy black. Always in the warm kitchen, amiably stirring sizzling pots: on a glowing with welcome range.

Or even learn to be comfortable bodies ourselves. But that again is asking too much from uncomfortable bodies like us. Neither one thing nor the other. Neither primitive nor civilized enough: to belong in either the kitchen or the sitting-room.

But at least we have thinned out considerably: the competitors to your marital favours. And there is no doubt that the Gentleman Farmer heads the list so far.

VIII

The Country to me is not a Haven of repose for the senile and dotty: as most Town people envisage it; in which to lay my weary bones, in lost-to-the-world retirement. But a growing crescendo of energy in the throbbing centre of my newfound world.

The Country is like a good woman abandoned for a bad woman: who is the Town. Who, though you despise her, holds you with her superficial evasions of your weakening initiative. Who makes it increasingly difficult for you to leave her precocious substitutes for living: of having it all done for you, instead of doing it yourself; in a fancy-dressed unreality.

Drugging the will: bemusing the senses; and killing outright the keen observer. Though your better, incarcerated nature, is parched dry. Longs to return to the thirst slaking Country of the good woman.

To whom: when at last your rallying weakness rebels against itself; and your mesmerized courage shakes itself: like a wet dog out of the beating down rain, shuddering into life again; you will, all the same, at your own prevaricating caprice: inescapably return.

But; although it is good and essential, for your Town-dulled observer: dying of a natural thirst; to return to the uncompromising Country: it is not an easy readjustment. Any more than it is an easy readjustment to return to an uncompromising good woman. After soaking in the lazy parasite charms of the Vampire woman's Town.

It will be a laborious process of solid, plodding uphill: climbing in boots of lead. Of barren expectation; Faithless waiting; and blindfold patience. Until the slow pulsing, Country muted rhythms; begin to beat haltingly again in your clogged-up blood. Unnoted as yet by you: your hearing still muffled in Town hostility.

The old harmonies will begin imperceptibly to readjust themselves. From your imprisoned nature propelled outwards; and free nature flowing inwards to fill the accommodating space. To meet each other again on a basis of equal friendliness.

The longer betrayal that you are away from nature; the longer will be the penitential trial: by which you get back to nature.

Once harmoniously re-established in the understanding of nature: your God will begin to breathe in you freely again. After his long bleak retirement in stifling Town apartments; where he could see no farther than the overshadowing trees in the crowded wood of people: in front of his stranger's face.

He will begin to grow in strength; to build independence in you. So that you will no longer be obligated; door-matted; or made to pay blood money to: any more soulsuckers of your displaced nature: at their mercy.

He will make you eventually: if you stick, leech undetachably, to his sole Creative guidance; sufficient unto yourself. Subjectively self supporting. Objectively unneedful of reinforcements from outside.

As proud and powerful as His own visible gifts of Country: laid out before your eyes. If your eyes are peeled to see them: for you to pick and choose from. As an exemplary map of the potential Country of your imagination. Of God's Country working through you; and your imagination working through God's Country. For your discrimination to do with: as it wills.

The explanation why the Townbred people can't stomach the overwhelming desolation of the Country: the lonely melancholy of too much endless unpeopled space; is that it shrivels up, and diminishes their personalities: by contrast.

They are closed in fearful denial against its incalculable size; so won't give it the initiatory time to percolate gradually into them. They only see the bare outlines of an austerely empty landscape. Frightening them back, at the double: to their home-town swarms of garrulousness.

Without stopping for an instant more, to feel the later, exchanged relationship that mellows with it. Or to listen to the underground mutterings; and chattily intimate whisperings: of its very personal language. For those who have ears lovingly open to hear. Who rock themselves in the songs of its changing weathers.

So, just as they, with their Town constriction of outlook: pity us, who belong to the Country: for our childishly ill-dressed children, shaming the suavity of their decorous streets, with their untrained gawkiness.

So we, who belong to the Country, with our, as it seems to us, broader outlook of the spreading countryside: pity their children for their scantily ill-dressed imaginations. Who have never been allowed the developing joy of playing naturally: in the revelling mud of nature.

Who have never had a preliminary period: dedicated to the fantasy flowering of Holy Childhood. Who leap, straight from the womb, into knowing Adulthood. With no transitional breakwaters of unknowing innocence.

Of infinitely precious Country innocence; that breaks our hearts: for us to break. That is hard as granite cliffs; and will not break. Will not be broken by the world's disillusions; nor split in two by humanity's corruptions.

Stands rock unbreakable: before Man's destructive contempt of innocence.

Therefore, always be profoundly grateful: Aeron from the Valley of the Aeron; that you have had God's greatest inheritance. Surpassing, by far, any future amount of stuffy universities: that of a childhood in the Country.

Notwithstanding, that you will deny your priceless Inheritance: over and over again. Get restless, and fed up: with the sleepy swaying and cradling of your youth; too high up in the solitary treetops.

Run away regularly to Town; to smash into jagged angles its unbroken pattern of time after time: the same monotonous illuminations of nature.

For nobody can stand illuminations: all the lit up time. There has got to be some dark foundation upon which to mount them: to set them off. Or how would the saints ever see their visions: without the contrast of lowliness that breeds visions. Without the dirt and grime in which visions flourish.

But, though you try perseveringly to obliterate: with every drowning submersion; your contained harvest of nature's brightness. You can only succeed temporarily.

It will always remain intact; held invisibly down inside you. For you to go back to: when you inevitably tire of submersion and subterfuge.

Which, sooner or later, you are bound to do: if you want to save the wilting crop of your untended, Country inheritance.

If you don't want to save it: you are not only massacring your most valuable possession. But massacring your original wholesomeness: in conjunction with it.

Lopping off the head of your healthily expanding God.

I do understand, all the same, only too well: having been once so abused myself a long time ago; that for a young girl to be named: 'A wholesome type'; is perhaps the deadliest insult of all. And she will do all that she extravagantly can do: to disabuse herself of the calumny of wholesomeness.

However, she will realize later on that it was an indispensable wholesomeness: to get her through her worst experiments in destructive vice.

With all my highflown blarneying about the bounteousness of the country: it is a little incongruous; and not a little humiliating; that I know informatively less: than the most ordinary bumpkin oaf. Who has no topographical idea; nor curious desire to find out: in what geographical strata of the boundless globe: he cud-chews his ditched life. Since his ditch of worshipped territory is his boundless globe.

Whose knowledge of nature is confined to an unreliable mixture of superstitious awe; and nicknamed inventions of his everyday, Country-cousin company. With no poor relation to correct Latin terminology.

Neither do I know one of the correct Latin names of the abundant flora that decorates: elbowing and jostling each other aside, to clear a rivalling passage of growth; the Country's thronging green surface.

And my abysmal knowledge of: The Gentle Art of Gardening; which I had been bargaining on: at the last casting off of ragbag affectations; is disgracefully insufficient.

Is, of all my numerous uncredited ignorances: my clown's joke of personified ignorance.

Bears no faint resemblance to my Mother's embroidered table cloth; with gentle Ladies, out of date, delicately tending tea roses. Fastidiously snipping at prickly bushes in rubber gloves: with pruning secateurs.

But, what if I do not possess those magical, plant coaxing, green fingers. If every seedling I heavy-weight touch, curls up wounded; and withers away pathetically.

What if my speciality is cutting down: with gusto. Instead of raising up: with a passion of patience.

For such accursed like me: black-fingered, root-perishing, reversals of nature; there is the vicarious compensation of the high inundating grass to be cut down. With a wildly sweeping, blunt scythe: spitefully slicing scars into more ankles than grass.

The enemy nettles: revengefully stinging the exposed flesh like a molested swarm of bees; to be hacked down among thc martyrcd apple trunks.

The recalcitrant weeds to be wrenched out, fighting: from their invasion of beds and paths; by the tough tendrils of their straggling hair.

The hawthorned, thorn-spiked at the ready, armoured hedges getting above themselves: to be attacked with a blade flashing sickle. Shaving off the profusion of stubble; steadily shaping into more presentable, thinned out, trimmed neatness of beard.

Which is a curative release of the clutch of captive nerves: climbing up the wall for a murderous outlet. If not precisely what is meant by: The Gentle Art of Gardening.

The pure eminence of the poverty-born Gardener: is the fierce, sackcloth shrouded from exposure, helmet hooded from the daylight, shy-of-the-light Islander. Who passionately presses and squeezes: out of a narrow ridge of inferior soil wedged between suffocating rocks; the squelching lusciousness that his deprivations crave.

He treats with that much more reverence; watches over with that much more solicitude; courts with that much more adoration: his meagre treasure of dusty soil; for the very reason of its meagreness.

With the just result that: from out of his grim Island of dry scarcity; he transforms its deficiencies into his solitary praying inspiration. Of that much more sensational beauty: because of its rarity. In the same category as the Latin: deprived of his native dreams; planting his lusciousness of tomatoes: in the desert in wartime.

What a dull figure by contrast: is the prosperous market gardener: with his flat acres of plenty.

IX

Now that we have arrived at this Terminal Point; in our journeying down the consecutive, dropping terraces of ominously advancing age; and landed: myself as an accomplished landing; but you, as an inconceivably distant nightmare landing; I want you to learn how to weather the universally oppressive: thunder cloud of loneliness.

Although I can never quite make out why: the terror of loneliness; should be a more shattering terror to old age: than to companionless youth. Whose thirst for company is surely more justifiably insistent: than the sated thirst of old age. Who, at least, has its once experienced companies: to people its loneliness.

I see no valid reason why old age should cut itself off more completely than youth: from its own generation of similarly cut off companions; in the same anchorless, flotsam drifting position. When each one of them, separately alone, is suffering the identical, despairing pangs: of discarded uselessness.

So why: in the name of commonsense; don't they get together, and chew the castigation of banishment: in sympathetic old company. Which, by sharing it, takes the cruel edge off the sharpness: of knifing inwards pain.

Instead of seeming to deliberately avoid: as though ashamed of them; their fellow sufferers in loneliness.

It is useless to say that they are left in loneliness

because all their old friends have died. Because; even if that is so; there are always plenty more old: new friends to be made.

But it is a queer thing that I have noticed: that old people don't like the company of other old people, like themselves. Perhaps it is too much like looking into an overbright mirror. A mirror which they would prefer to be blurred over by the fly's droppings of younger days.

It makes all the subtle difference to your susceptibilities; what name you give to a State of Being. For instance, if you call your ignoble loneliness: Wilful Solitude; it takes on entirely another, nobler aspect. Which has the added assuagement to your vanity of being: of your own Egotist choosing. Whether it is honestly your choice: or deceptively a Public Face saver.

Such an honest choice of: Wilful Solitude; carries with it, at its peak best: disregarding for now, the price-paying bleaknesses involved; an arrogant pride of solitary achievement. Which scorns any dignity lowering, human support: in its Bamboo splintering Pyramid of self-aggrandisement.

But there is always the imminent peril: of sliding off the perilous brink of your Pyramid of Solitude. Which then cracks up once more into lowly deteriorating loneliness.

So it is pessimistically wiser: since pessimism as a foregone victor, defeats optimism with predictable regularity; and, whatever pessimistic defeat is anticipated, is outclassed by an ambushed unanticipated, and therefore more shocking one; to prophetically envisage the inevitable lowering of your pride-keyed Pyramid. To admit your humbling need for company: at some unpredictable stage of uncertainty.

To admit that even vainglorious you: smothered in your

adolescence of false impregnability; at some unpremeditated time; in some unguarded, failing-of-Faith dejection; some sinking to the organic dregs period of morbid mood; will have a child's crying need for the nearness; the comforting warmth of the proximity: of the once scorned presence, of other, communal bodied people: near you.

If it is only to sandbag you up again: by surrounding you with their muddy trench of humanity; in your Hermitage of Denial.

For, there is nothing quite so offensively galling, as doing a big: Rejection of Common Circulation Act; that is crassly unnoticed, blandly ignored: by that very self-same rejected Common Circulation.

Who: though fathoms beneath your unique notice; should at least have the common decency, the elementary manners: to notice your uniqueness. To be suitably impressed, or rudely shocked: by your daring of difference from them.

Your brave Act of Rejection. Put on, with the underlying shielded, but unmistakable showing off purpose: of confounding, and spurring them into retaliation. By retaliating on you with furious opposition and loud condemnation.

Furious opposition and loud condemnation is what you are provoking them for. What your acting feeds and thrives upon. Since any attention: to the born putter on of Acts; is better than none. And the more condemnatory the attention; the better will be your Act: in opposition to it.

So: though so pettily Plebeian in your scoffing eyes; the Plebeians are your undeniable, nectar-distilling audience. Without whom, you can't perform with the dramatic inspiration of outrage. If there is no audience of the 'ordinary': to be extraordinarily outraged against.

Without whom it is hardly worth the sacrificial sweat

of your Hermitage. With no open-mouthed audience: to applaud your extraordinary sacrifice.

Whether the applause is approval, or disapproval, is immaterial to the chronic Actor. Who is intoxicated only by their prodded roar of disturbance. Roaring in his singing ears.

But disapproval nevertheless, gives to his performance: an added zest. A stoned martyr's stones of compassion. To hurl back at them.

Whereas approval softens it down; tends to turn his passion lukewarm: into petering out repetition.

Even the most ingrown toenailed Hermit must have his audience: upon whom to spit his contempt. Or else he might as well be a plain, contemptible, mass looker-on himself: at the phenomenal exception.

As opposed to being an exceptional Actor staging his own original play.

He need not worry that his precious exception will be effaced in company. Because: even if he tries to lose himself in company; he will still remain alone. The company will but accentuate his exception: his lost to them isolation.

So you have got to choose early: whether to be lost in company; and thus attain peaceful mediocrity.

Or whether to weather loneliness: to fight through all its beating down weathers; and thus attain isolation aloft. Or isolation below, as the case may be.

But, having chosen the latter alternative: I should advise peaceful mediocrity, as much more tolerable. Bearing in mind as well: that there is always mediocre isolation, to be contended with.

For the two together are not compatible. But your isolation aloft will allow you the possibility of dabbling in company: with a sharp eye mentally annotating every libellous detail. In the private manner of that excellent exponent of mental annotation: Mr. John Malcolm Brinnin. While at the same time: unlike the lost in company; not being involved in company.

So take my tip: miserable as it is; Look and Learn. As an improving motto to: Live and be Killed.

Sham social elasticity: while quietly tying up the squeezing knots of your observations out of sight.

It is nice to be nice: as we all know; but it is nicer still: to be clever.

I will tell you this too: that 'being clever' is something that can be learnt. It is not something that one is necessarily born with. Learnt from somebody being cleverer than oneself.

From somebody, if you like: making a fool out of you. So that you are stung into making a nastier fool out of them. A debunked fool: by your barbed cleverness.

There is no place for the fool. Especially a Gargantuan fool like I was. Before I learnt to be a bit cleverer: at fooling my foolers. By making out: only too easily; to still be the fooled fool myself.

But only the exceptional fool can afford the luxury of: playing the fool. So that, when you fall flat on your face, you can say: I was only fooling, you fool.

X

Let me now shove the old organic burning boat back into its rotting port. And take a vertiginous leap up into the giddy air of mundane play-acting again. Play-act while you can, for it is one of the prerogatives of youth: that it can afford to forget the organic burning up of age.

And, take it from me, if you wish to live with a man in harmony while you can: there is no other way but play-acting. Then, every now and then, to your fearful consternation, the play-acting will come alive: and you will be no longer play-acting. But it is essential that he cannot detect which is which.

Never be so simple as to seek for happiness: it is not a bird that you can put in a cage. By so doing you will only clip its wings.

If happiness comes at all: which is by no means prearranged; it comes by the way, while you are seeking for something else. Something outside yourself, beyond yourself: in a brief absorption of self-forgetfulness. And, when it comes, you probably won't recognize it, till afterwards. By contrast with your bitter tasting self absorption again.

But always aspire higher than you can. For, however high you aspire: you will never arrive more than halfway up the cliff of your aspiration.

I dread to think in what grovelling toad mire you would arrive; if you aspired lower than you can. Which is what it sometimes looks like I have done.

It is a case of pushing the brain beyond its insufficient limitations: by the sheer desire to excel.

Then, precisely through the very humiliation of your insufficiency; and, as a challenge to the pain it has cost you: you will make a garment of your own.

An awkward clumsy thing at first, but an original model. From which, furthering of the best of your ability, you will have excelled.

And always keep, as a golden habit, not only the door of your house, but the door of your heart, ajar: for the unknown stranger. Who might be, you never know: in whatsoever ludicrous, Barbary ape shape he appears; the faultily made 'Christ' for you.

Because: although you may foolishly long for the perfectly made 'Christ' for you; to the imperfect the perfect is too dazzling. Perfection wipes out imperfection with its blinding light.

So that imperfect people like us need a 'Christ' as faultily imperfect as ourselves, if not more so. Beside whom we can shine with our own light, intensified in his reflected light.

Whose bristling back of spiked faults will complement and blunt the spikes of yours. Making them seem, comparatively, stunted nothings; next to his overshadowing ones.

Making you into a crowned Queen of shining virtue: as compared to him. Which is surely preferable; more reassuring to your touchy vanity; than being made into a prostrate, blinded, sack of sins: by your ideal 'Christ'.

But, who is to know, but you, where, in whom, in what unlikely mis-shape, your true 'Christ' resides.

So you must always seek for him everywhere, in everybody. For, even the totally ugly, repulsive stranger, holds some buried relic of 'Christ': behind his repulsion of aspect. A relic that you can excavate out of him, and make abundance of. That will serve you better; for your personal pains and human efforts: than a playboy of saintliness. Who, as the pay-off for his faultlessness, is unavoidably: a crashing bore into the bargain.

Is it not more sensible then: for an irretrievably impure sinner, to seek another irretrievably impure sinner, like themselves; and get on with it together, the best they can. Helping each other with the charity of a tolerant 'Christ', who understands their special weaknesses: their mutual sins of indulgence.

As an 'Alcoholic Anonymous' helps his twin Alcoholic Anonymous: through the sympathy of the same shared weakness. Building up incognito together: their weak outcast army of fluctuating will power; against the insidious temptations of drink.

Not by being untouchably high; high above the clouds of sin so high; will the sinner listen to sense.

For the high and mighty sun, at high noon, scorches him up. Is too far outside his scope of sun: through darkened glasses. Too far outside his arm-length reach.

No, it is better for the pariah dog sinner in the dark, to stick to his own mongrel breed. Fitting snugly together in their doghouse in disgrace.

Rather than to attempt to balance, on his lousy head, an incongruous halo, sitting absurdly askew.

For, the further and the faster, he runs from a feared reality: the more fearful will be its bite, when it catches up with him.

Fearful as reality is: it is less fearful than evasions of reality.

So it is useless to evade reality, because it only makes it more virulent in the end. But instead, look steadfastly into the slit, pin-pointed, malignant eyes of reality: as an old-hand trainer dominates his wild beasts.

Take it by the scruff of the neck, and shake the evil intent out of it; till it rattles out harmlessly, like gall bladder stones, fossilized on the floor.

From facing and dominating reality, you will then have taken the whiplash of fear out of it.

You will then be in charge of reality; and can do what you like with it. Instead of reality being in charge of you; and doing what it likes with you.

As fearlessly as you must learn to dominate the wild beast of reality, so that you are not afraid of it any more; so you must learn to dominate the people in your reality, so that you are not afraid of them any more.

For the people: whether you court, or run away from them; are the universe; and the universe is your dearly beloved, indispensable life blood.

It is a fallacy, I believe, to say that, with the power of domination, automatically follows a domineering tyranny. From what I have seen of genuinely powerful people; people of authentic integrity; the sure existence of their assurance in themselves, does the opposite. Allows them: because they are no longer aggressively afraid, or aggressively competing; to be tolerantly charitable.

You must have the proximity, the nearness, the smell, the warmth: the noise of people. But not the stifling of their actual presences on top of you all the time. Too much people, in an anonymous city, can be as solitarily assassinating: as not enough people, in a lonely village. Only by periodic communion with people: mixing and interchanging of your country's wine, with their country's wine; will your wine; watered down in too much isolation; gain enrichment of new body.

So now: Aeron the Byron; at the winding up of your Epilogue: poke your bright fire on. The Byronic tower is out; and the communal mixing bowl is in.

Have done with circumspection. Forget about dissimulation. And throw that odious, smirking, stuffed peacock: moderation; who is always self righteously right; who always knows when he has had enough; who always retires at the diplomatic moment: with his complacent sneer of superiority over your excessive extremes; toppling, tight-arse-over-trembling tip, overboard.

Give your curbed horses: on this final winning stretch, their uncurbed, mane-tossing heads.

The extent that you will permit yourself this liberation: will depend on the size of the wodge of money behind you. That both holds you up: and sets you up; as on a raised oak lavatory on top of a skyscraper. Looking down on the improvident, unprovided for, less well-endowed streaming mud of humanity.

That will put you at the talking head of the file: instead of at the mute tail.

This wodge pile of splendour, will give you not only the resplendent glory of rolling in it; but the uniquely effective firearm for action: power. Without which firearm: action is ineffectual.

It is a heady and dangerous position; but the sole, solitary position worth being in. Late in life, however, when you have learned how to use it wisely.

For only late in life, can you use the teaching of hardships to constructive advantage. And, if you have learned well in your apprentice lifetime, you will do well in your governing lifetime.

The prior knowledge of the unpleasant side of life, is essential to the proper appreciation of the luxurious innovations.

This is why I think that the parvenu is likely to know better; and to handle better: the value of power. Since he has had a longer time, while sweating for it: to think about how best, most enterprisingly, to dispose of it.

Than the dead fish born into power, who hardly notices it, or thinks of making use of it. But takes for jaded granted his safeguarding safes of unenterprising power.

You will be able to afford now too the luxury: of being sensationally extravagant with your personality. Of turning it into whatever sensation of extravagance takes your whim, or caprice. Sensationally difficult, or sensationally nice, by turn.

The luxury of really enjoying yourself for the first time. Not as you are supposed to enjoy yourself by conventional custom: but as you have always wanted to, but never had the courage to, previously.

You will learn the profound differences: between paying your own whack; and having your own whack paid for. Or not having any whack to pay.

The profound difference in being a respected member of a paying institution; as opposed to being the ultimate nail in the coffin of unpaying institutions.

The profound difference: between depending on friends' unpaid hospitality; or depending on the paid hospitality of your own choosing. There is no comparable question of which is the more pleasant.

I have progressively found, what is more, that by paying people: for company, or looking after you, or even loving you; they do it a lot more willingly, more conscientiously: than those who are morally bound to do it. Than those who do it through bonds of family obligation, or sentimental attachment.

For their resentment, and consequent hostility: for being morally held down, and morally made to do it for nothing; is blatantly visible to an objective observer.

The family, most particularly, is the brittlest, most easily breakable staff to lean on: enough to gently lean on it, and it snaps promptly in two. It can only remain intact, so long as you are careful never to lean on it.

Whereas, in a straightforward paying arrangement for services rendered: there are none of those unprepossessing repercussions of swallowed loathing: that come out in all nagging manner of pinching digs, and poking prods of revenge.

But, as for my mudraking self; powerful as is my desire to get into your wealthy society; my desire to keep out: for my own self protection; is even more powerful.

So I must leave this enviable social position: for your more resilient wits to conquer. Stick to my mud; and venture out at planned festive intervals, to visit your high life.

Ideally I can see us: as gay, elegant and amusing as Lady Docker: lapping up pink bubbly all day long on our luxury yacht; with a continual string orchestra nostalgically stringing us along: in rippling eddies of hiccuping gaiety.

But, it is no good: you can't turn a mudpat into a crystal decanter. So: when the ball is over; I shall return to my Cinderella world; where, in the obscurity of: Muzio Clementi; my most musical distractions are listening to the clicking of the policemen's billiard cues at night. To remind themselves that: in spite of every evidence to the contrary, an insect of endeavour scratches within them. Or listening to the reproving clicking of the landlady's heels, in the flat above me, in the unspeakable hours of horribly early morning. To remind me that: virtuous 'she' has something to do; even if degenerate me has not.

There is this to be said for the principles of Christianity: which are a whole philosophy of survival made for the poor; that by saying to oneself often enough, and believing it enough, that: water is wine; it does, in its delicious descent, turn into wine.

I have experimented myself, in circumstances of poverty: where automatically develops, simply because there is not, a famished appetite; this metamorphosizing of a common foodstuff or liquid: into an uncommon exotic one.

My findings were successful: a plain potato became an exquisite feast of delicacy. A vinegar sour wine became the rarest of ancient vintages: or very nearly so: because my believing capacity was not all that good.

On the same system of word suggestion, the Italians, from long poverty, by always putting 'bella' before whatever insufficiency they have got to eat: make it that much more appetizing.

But, let us remember, when choosing our God: that the crying need for a God in all of us; does not necessarily create one: to suit us all.

It is best to take a bit of each person's God; and mould it to your God's will.

But what is truly beautiful, to my calculating avarice, in the overflow orgy in the confessional: is that you don't have to pay for it.

Not to have to pay nowadays, for the joy of an intimate spouting out of oneself: is Christian in its true pristine sense.

Much has been made in dirt manufacturing, juice distilling, literature: on the lasciviousness of Priests. On the sexual orgies resulting from it: under the hypocritical cloak of their vowed celibacy. The more heinously erotic, by reason of their chained celibacy blasting through the cast-iron taboos of the Sacred Law.

Much, I would venture to guess: having no proof one way or another; that is grossly exaggerated. Because there is nothing the infidel delights in more than casting slurs on the good faith of the faithful. In disproving their authenticity of purpose; and showing up the vile corruption that lies beneath the disguise of purity.

But this vile corruption, that they condemn so indignantly; and illustrate with lurid, mostly fictional examples; is much much more likely to be; is prevalently more present: in the corrupt envy of the beholder.

For every corrupt abuser of the Faith: there is a volcano prevalence of Faithful.

It is at the last panting lap of the breaking-up of the body: of the rattling of the ashes to cinders; that the reckoning up of how much spent, and how much put aside: takes place implacably. Not in the Everlasting Gardens of panic contrived Afterlife.

And the soul: suffocated in the body's meaty folds; punch drunk from its battery of beatings; finally blinks open its bleary jellied gaze: and comes back into its own judgement ring.

For those who have treated it with respect; fed it well; regularly attended to all its delicate fads and fancies: it gracefully bestows the inestimable reward of Serenity.

Never having experienced myself this benign state, it is difficult to explicitly define: in what specific elements it consists. But, at a sweeping attempt, I would guess: that it is primarily a maturity, which inevitably brings with it a ghastly resignation. This resignation in turn entails, for its efficacity, a Saint's superlative selflessness. Which means a total extermination of the vanity of play-acting. Without which I find it hard to envisage living; which must then become, I can't help feeling: a lukewarm bath lacking in bath salts. But only by thus draining all the salt out of the sea: can you gain a still and tranquil lake of Serenity.

This must explain why we are not as yet serene; why we cling, for dear life, to our play-acting; and, even on the grassy verge of the ultimate abyss, will be busily putting on our: dying duck in a thunderstorm; faces.

It is safer in your own favour to accept the proffered Act at its face value. For whoever has the temerity to delve beneath the face: to peer through the ravaged barriers and prick on a pin the worm wriggling soul; merits the Viper that bites him.

There is another snag attached to Serenity for the would-be creative person; which can be both an advantage and a disadvantage. That: while basking in the release of preoccupation with self, it evolves a detached clarity of vision. Which sees, frightfully clearly, the puniness of self in proportion to the universe. So that, although its vision is larger; it simultaneously eliminates the presumption to create. And it is that essential presumption we must cling on to like sea-wrecked castaways: if we intend to create a raft.

That is why we fight to retain our vain density of vision: which sees the puniness of the universe in proportion to us. Otherwise how could we drive our matchstick stakes into it.

What is the purpose, I would like to know: of being an unstruck match in a multiple matchbox. We want to take our matches out and strike them: if only for the pleasure of seeing them burn up.

So, I fear: Serenity is out for us incendiaries.

Upon those on the other, left hand of the soul: who have consistently denied its internal eminence; refused to slake its thirsts; pressed it down, like shiny fish's roes in a tin; it wreaks an arid desert of desolation. A wreaking of chronic discontent. No matter what soft mattresses are put under it, or silken shawls wrapped around it. A perpetual rag gnawing of doubt: which gnaws through the fattest, featherstuffed, goosiest eiderdowns.

It is in this desert then of desolation, discontent, and doubt; that the scum of the soul, shrunken in disrepute; wanders aimless, strays abandoned, forever searches: in a blind wilderness of the body: for the way out.

Besides which your formal Hell of roasting on sizzling coals, is positively cosy.

It is now too then: when the body is counted out; when the soul has come into its tardy ascendancy: and is gloating, like a callous schoolboy, over the body's abject fall from grace; that the call for help: when no help is near; will go unheard.

Now: in this climate of pain; at this desperate hour; that the wail for the saving salves of the black beetle doctors of the soul: will begin in vain.

With the curling up of youth: like a sea horse skeleton; the lowering of sailing hopes, hot ambitious prides; the surrender of stiff dignities, pompous pretensions; as a last fearful resource, is sought, too late: the sheltering wings of the black beetle's church. An older brother's church; which the prodigal lost soul omitted to give a hand in building. But runs to, in extremity, to house its mounting fears: for lack of a lifetime of loyalty to it: from the beginning. But, for all its recent ardour of necessity conversion, its Faith does not compete, in spiritual value; with the training of a lifetime in the formulas of Faith. With one born in the hereditary blood of the church.

Nevertheless: in this sand of the desert; in this climate of pain: where a momentary lifting of its steamed-down lid is a revelation in the sky; there is a redeeming feature. For there are hidden: very deep down, to be sure, and sparsely sown: the tiny seeds of creation. But it takes a desperately keen ferret to ferret them out. Since its only negative stimulus is to annihilate its surrounding aridity: by sowing over its thickets of shady trees. If only to make for itself, at least a patch: of shade to sit in.

I ought to know; because I have lived long enough in this playground of light and shade: to know how important it is to get rid of the light.

The reason, I have decided, why people don't screech their heads off night and day; when arrived at this terminal, no turning back, climax stage of existence; when envisaging: except that they mule refuse to envisage it for themselves; the inexorably repeated sequence of living then after dying over and over again: flaunting mortality before them; menacing them down the mortal ages; is that, like the prisoner in the condemned cell, having accepted death as an accomplished fact: there is nothing more to lose.

Hence their seemingly irrelevant frivolity; their childish whimsicality at this dreaded termination. Which for them, in mind, is already terminated.

The real anguish is all enacted in the passageway between life and death. In the sun beckoning through the bars of the cell. In the conflict of longings. In the pulling forward towards the light, counterbalanced by: the pulling backward towards the shade. In the deadlocked tug of war.

There you are then: after all this gassy palavering, and prating preachings to you: my favourite daughter, with no hesitation. There is no other. Pure undiluted Thomas milky pigmentation on top. From your milk running hands: to your spilt milk feet. But with enough Macnamara blood underneath: grumbling and rumbling in your blue swollen veins; to launch a thousand battleships.

Back on the love lark again: counting the cherry stones on the side of your plate. Loves me; loves me not; loves me . . . Got to finish on loves me; or sneak another stone in when nobody's looking.

Loves me a little; loves me a lot; loves me passionately; loves me to madness; loves me not at all . . . Can't possibly end there. Must quickly reassemble the stones: to madness.

Now who can this paragon of all diamonds be: who loves you to madness.

Tinker.
Tailor.
Soldier.
Sailor.
Rich man.
Poor man.
Beggar man.
Thief.

Since there is but one desirable match among this low bunch; it is going to be quite a job to make the capricious stones combine to point unswervingly to: Rich man. And, knowing the excess of your perversity: and if only for the joy of opposing your poor mother's dying wishes; you will treacherously point to the next door down the street: Poor man. If not: out of pure stubborn cussedness, to: Beggar man. Or, at least less penuriously to: Thief.

But think thrice: my whippersnapper; count seven: before you allow your romantic fancy to run away with you. Because: be warned by one who knows the worst; it is not the man you marry. But his tidily packed: in long accumulated layers; baggage.

With which baggage: however monstrously old is the hide of it; there is nothing insuperable to stop you: from purchasing the poor man of your deluded dreams. Whose blooming, as the hawthorn in May, beauty: had you picked him penniless; would very soon have faded into: a freezing up of the pipes in winter.

So let your phantom bridegroom be more richly lined;

and caparisoned from within. A man of inner, invisible substance. Rather than a tangible bridegroom: seductively embellished from without. A man of dangling ding dong parts: flapping all over the shop.

Are you ready then. Let's try once more. One; two; three: off you go . . .
Tinker.
Tailor.
Soldier.
Sailor.
Rich man. STOP.

But perhaps the word I am after is not: Love; after all. There is too much emphasis on: Love; altogether. Perhaps it is endurance. It is about time that soft meaningless word: Love; was taken out of the dictionary. So that instead of saying: I will love you for ever; it would be a much more convincing proof to say: I will endure you for ever. For what is there left but to endure: what is left.

Here ends the Last Lesson, with the only prayer that is worth making: Give me strength for what I have to do. Although to whom the prayer is made, God only knows. The fact that, at any moment, the one who prays so fervently for strength to act: is liable to be swallowed up by the earthworms; does not detract from the intensity of his prayer. For the poor simpleton is not able to relate: the strength of his fervour to the futility of his fervour. Luckily for them. And that goes for me too.

It all ends on a prayer not of my making. Teach me to care and not to care. Teach me to sit still. Caring and not caring is child's play. But what is: sitting still; but acute endurance.

As a last purge for you to swallow is: the more you do, the more you can do. As inversely, the less you do, the less you can do. So keep going: even if you have got no lighted indication of where to go.

To be asleep: or to be awake; is the question. Best of all Aeron: to be awake. Even though you *look*: my angel sleeping.

Your almost sleeping: but not
angelically; Mother.